W9-BRM-853

Sor Juana Inés de la Cruz

Sor Juana Inés de la Cruz

Religion, Art, and Feminism

Pamela Kirk

CONTINUUM • NEW YORK

1998
The Continuum Publishing Company
370 Lexington Avenue
New York, NY 10017

Printed in the United States of America

Library of Congress Cataloging-in-Publication Data

Kirk, Pamela.
    Sor Juana Inés de la Cruz : religion, art, and feminism /Pamela
Kirk.
       p. cm.
    Includes bibliographical references and index.
    ISBN 0-8264-1043-X (hardback : alk. paper)
    1. Juana Inés de la Cruz, Sister, 1651–1695—Criticism and interpre-
tation. 2. Christianity in literature. 3. Women and literature—
Mexico—History—17th century. 4. Feminism in literature. 5. Theology,
Doctrinal—Mexico—History—17th century. 6. Catholic Church—
Doctrines—History—17th century. I. Title
PQ7296.J6Z692 1998
861—DC21   97-17272
                                                        CIP
                                                        r97

❧

To my parents
Mary S. and Robert J. Kirk
in love and admiration

Contents

Acknowledgments

I am indebted to many people over the years of working on this book: first to Ernest Ranly C.P.P.S. who introduced me to the contemporary church in Latin America and its pre-Columbian past on an extended visit to Peru in 1988; to my friends Teresa Mendez Faith (St. Anselm College) and Lorraine Roses (Wellesley College), professors of Spanish literature who encouraged me in my study of Sor Juana; to María Pilar Aquino, Ada María Isasi Díaz, and Jeanette Rodriguez for their interest, support, and constructive criticism.

St. John's University has been generous in support of my research with teaching reductions and a summer research grant without which my work would not have been posssible.

I am especially grateful to Justus George Lawler, my editor, whose cordiality and generous criticism has brought the book to completion. The bibliographic acumen and attentive proofreading of my assistant, Kate von Braunsberg, smoothed the way on many occasions. Frances Fico has been invaluable in shepherding the manuscript through various revisions with her computer skills, her calm and her invariable good humor.

To my brother Robert, who helped me navigate the Library of Congress; to Susan, my sister, who took me to Sanborns where I discovered Sor Juana; and to her daughter, my niece, Danielle Abeyta who embodies a triple heritage, Hispanic, Native American, and European; to my sister Ellen; and especially to my parents Mary and Robert for their years of encouragement—my heartfelt gratitude.

Introduction

Why would a seventeenth-century Mexican nun, Sor Juana Inés de la Cruz, be the subject of a feature film, _Yo la peor de todas_ (I, the worst of all), by Argentina's most famous woman director, María Luisa Bemberg, in 1990? Why has a playwright such as Antonio Arenas, whose _The Phoenix of the New World_ caused a minor sensation at Paris' Théâtre Odéon in the summer of 1992, been inspired to dramatize her life?[1] What about her life and accomplishments led the Mexican government to put her portrait on the 200-pesos bill? Why did the 1990 exhibit "Mexico, Splendor of Thirty Centuries" at New York's Metropolitan Museum of Art contain a near-life-size portrait of Sor Juana? Why would New York City's Hispanic theater festival devote one evening to a reading of her work in the summer of 1993? Why is Sor Juana Inés de la Cruz generating dozens of scholarly articles and books in several disciplines and numerous languages? Why did _Academe,_ the American Association of University Professors' bimonthly bulletin, select her name as one of the four women engraved on the "new temple of learning" in its cover photograph, when featuring a feminist revision of the literary canon? Mexico's own Nobel Prize–winning poet, Octavio Paz, provides only a partial answer to these questions in his groundbreaking biography of Sor Juana when he rates her among the first five lyric poets of the Spanish language. The fact that even high school students in Latin America today, at the mention of Sor Juana's name, immediately recite the first lines of "Hombres nescios" (Foolish men), her satirical poem on "the double standard," points to another explanation of her recent popularity among scholars and a more general public: few figures embody more profoundly the ambivalent integration of educated women in society and culture.

There is another dimension to Sor Juana that has received minimal attention among all this: her religious writings, which comprise two-thirds of her total work. These are the primary focus of my investigation. For the most part they occupy a middle place between literature and theology. They can be difficult for a theologian because of their poetic and dramatic form. Conversely the literary scholar often lacks the background of the general religious culture of the seventeenth century which is taken for granted in Sor Juana's work. Part of my task has been to examine Sor Juana's religious works from a new point of view by taking into consideration the literary dimension for theologians and by illuminating the religious background for literary scholars. However, this book is also intended to introduce Sor Juana to a nonspecialist as a significant religious figure who was not just accidentally a woman, but who consciously incorporated as major components in her work concerns which today's scholars term "feminist."

When I first encountered Sor Juana in Mexico City in August of 1989, I was browsing in the book section at Sanborns on the Avenida Reforma, vaguely conscious of that mix of impressions which characterize visits to foreign bookstores: print of a different smell, paper of unaccustomed texture, cultural icons in familiar frames with different faces. On the cover of one book a woman's face emerged out of a dark background. It was the portrait of a beautiful nun. The luxurious white sleeves of her habit contrasted with its simple black veil. A shieldlike medallion covered her neck and chest. This was my first glimpse of Paz' *Sor Juana Inés de la Cruz o las trampas de la fe* (published in English translation as *Sor Juana; or, The Traps of Faith*) and my purchase of this book marked the beginning of a process of discovery and disclosure which has come to characterize my experience of her work.[2]

Now eight years later I continue to be astonished by this woman who was able to educate herself in what was nearly a frontier outpost to become the accepted partner of leading thinkers and ecclesiastical authorities of her cultural world. In one of her treatises she competes with the most eminent Mexican scholar of her day, Carlos Sigüenza y Góngora. In another she challenges the most famous Latin American writer of her century, the Brazilian/Portuguese Jesuit Antonio de Vieira. In a third she defends her devotion to learning and the intellectual life to a neighboring bishop who has criticized her in print. In another letter she dismisses her confessor, the Jesuit Nuñez de Miranda, because of his malicious gossip about her intellectual activities.

Sor Juana breaks the stereotype of the writer nun in other ways. Nearly all her religious writings are intended to reach beyond the convent walls. Her religious poetry was written to be sung in the cathedrals of Mexico City, Puebla, and Oaxaca. Her religious dramas were composed with a view to their being performed in the courts of Mexico City or Madrid. The longest of her most typical devotional works, *Exercises for the Feast of the Incarnation* is intended for a mixed audience, including priest, nuns, and laity. Her writings are not mystical, nor even with one or two rare exceptions, examples of private devotion. They radiate, however, with an exuberance which is characteristic of a vibrant faith able to survive in trying circumstances. The range of forms (poetry, drama, scholarly disputation, autobiography) which Sor Juana manipulates with confidence, ease, and skill are unequalled, with the possible exception of the twelfth-century abbess Hildegard of Bingen.

As a result of the public nature of her religious writings, I will not be examining in any detail Sor Juana's relationships with women she knew. This includes the countess of Paredes, whom I will consider only as Sor Juana's patroness without exploring the dimensions of the friendship of the two women which has led to considerable (and inconclusive) speculation based on some of Sor Juana's poems addressed to the countess. These poems are not part of Sor Juana's religious work, and therefore are not under consideration here. I will, however, be taking care to consider the writings of the men with whom Sor Juana interacted in order to give the reader a sense of the degree to which Sor Juana was their equal, or even their superior in logical argumentation, breadth of culture, and brilliance of language.

RELIGION

MY INTEREST IN Sor Juana's religious works and my perspective as a theologian, as I have said, will necessarily provide a different angle of vision on her work than that of literary scholars. This became evident to me when I returned to Paz's *Sor Juana; or, The Traps of Faith* after reading Sor Juana's works. I was surprised by his condescending attitude toward her theology:

> It is not easy to take her theological opinions very seriously; rather than deep convictions, they were brilliant

speculations to be uttered in a lecture hall, in the locutory
of a convent, or on the stage of a theater. What interested
her was to present herself in the best possible light.[3]

This great admirer of Sor Juana seemed willing to allow for her
excellence in private, personal forms of literary activity, such as lyric
poetry, but had difficulty admitting her to weightier matters such as
politics, theology, or philosophy.

Obviously I do not share Paz's negative assessment of the
weight of Sor Juana's theological reflections. Startling is the evidence of the concerns of today's theologies running like invisible
threads through her work, forming patterns of connection between
then and there and now and here. Among these are her concern for
the process of evangelization and her sensitivity to the mingling of
cultures, her exploration of Mary as a figure of power, and her incor-
poration of the voices of the poor into her religious celebrations.

ART

FROM THE OUTSET I wish to affirm my indebtedness to the research
and analysis of literary scholars, and acknowledge their insights.[4]
This is all the more necessary in Sor Juana's case because the theological content to be considered is for the most part embodied in
literary forms—poetry and plays—rather than in straightforward
prose. The more than two hundred lyric poems classified in the first
volume of her collected works[5] bear witness to Sor Juana's command of the sonnet, the romance, the epigram, and to other more
specifically Spanish verse forms. The major portion (twelve cycles of
eight poems) of her explicitly religious poetry are liturgical compositions called *villancicos*, a type of solemn vespers sung in the cathedral in Spanish, containing dialogues, folk figures, humor, and
satire. Her dramas include three full-length sacramental dramas
(*autos*), two comedies, and over fifteen one-act plays (*loas*). The
description of a triumphal arch dedicated to the viceroy, a theological treatise in the form of an autobiographical letter, a retreat in the
form of a novena, prayers to be said for communal meditation of
the Rosary, and three short pieces confirming her religious commitment make up the body of her prose.

This remarkable variety of literary expression offers a challenge
to the theologian because of contemporary expectations of the
genre of theological discourse as prose reflection and critical argumentation. Sor Juana's age was accustomed to receiving religious

content not only through sermons, works of theology, and books of devotion, but also through sacramental dramas publicly performed especially for the feast of Corpus Christi, and musical minidramas presented in the liturgy of major feasts. Because she was adept at using these popular forms, consideration of her theology from this angle can also be instructive for the theology of our time in its search for alternative expressions of theological content.

Sor Juana's religious poetry and drama were designed to reach a broader audience than her secular love lyrics written for the viceregal court, and they represented the more "popular" segment of her work. Ironically they are less accessible to the twentieth-century reader because the secularization of our own popular culture has depleted and impoverished the grid of religious referents available to us.

FEMINISM

STUDIES HAVE SHOWN that the marginalized have access to public discourse in forms which are themselves considered marginal. Sor Juana is no stranger to this insight and part of her defense of herself against the criticism that she had overstepped the boundaries appropriate for a woman was that nearly all of her work was "poetry" and as such was not weighty enough to be subject to the Inquisition, although subject to the sometimes painful arbitration of good taste.

• Literary scholars of the last two decades have embarked on a feminist rereading of Sor Juana which has revealed the nun's commitment to the dignity of women as a central element of nearly every major work. One early example is "Sor Juana Explores Space" in *Plotting Women: Gender and Representation in Mexico*,[6] an essay which brilliantly analyzes her "social location" in the viceregal court and in the colonial church. As a woman in a patriarchal society, as an educated woman in a convent where women's education was private and haphazard, Sor Juana was a "fairground freak . . . who was constantly on show, exhibited . . . as a 'rare bird' because she was a woman who wrote on religious matters and a nun who wrote profane poetry."[7] More recently two collections of essays explore multiple dimensions: *Feminist Perspectives on Sor Juana,* edited by Stephanie Merrim in 1991, and *Υ diversa de mí misma entre vuestras plumas ando* (And different from myself I wander among your words), a volume of papers presented in Mexico at an international conference in her honor in 1993.[8]

* * *

I HAVE TRIED to let the content of Sor Juana's work govern my presentation. The occasional nature of her work, its embeddedness in literary forms, escapes neat categorization into traditional theological topics (Christology, ecclesiology, eschatology). As a result I have opted not to force the religious dimension of her writing into standard theological categories. To do so would truncate what in her work is unusual, such as her interest in evangelization, mission, the interaction of cultures, and the process of the conversion of the Americas.

A second major concern is to acquaint readers with Sor Juana's own voice by summary and by close analysis of key texts. Nearly all of the longer texts I will be considering have not been translated in their entirety, and only one, *Response to Sor Philotea de la Cruz,* exists in recent and accessible translations.[9] Though I will be considering primarily works that have explicitly religious content, even with this limitation I cannot hope for completeness since nearly two-thirds of over two thousand pages in the critical edition of Sor Juana's work falls into this category.[10]

1

Points of Departure

Not to be born of an honorable father would be a blemish, I must own . . . [1]

(OC 1:492)

Given my complete disinclination to matrimony . . . [the convent] was the least inappropriate and most decent path I could choose . . . to work out my salvation.

(OC 4:271–73)

BORN IN SAN MIGUEL NEPANTLA, a small village at the foothills of the volcano Popocatépetl, about "ten leagues" from Mexico City in 1648, Juana Inés Ramírez de Asbaje spent her early childhood years on her grandfather's hacienda and fed her precocious intellectual appetite by reading books from his library. Through family connections she was sent to the capital to further her education. Her lively intellect, beauty, and vivacious personality attracted the attention of court circles. The vicereine, Leonor Carreto, marquise of Mancera, brought her into the court as her lady in waiting, probably in 1664. In August of 1667 she entered the Carmelite convent of San José, but left after three months, apparently because the rigid discipline of the reformed Carmelites was too hard on her health. In February of 1669 she became a professed nun of the Hieronimite order in the convent of St. Paula, never again to leave its confines. The limitations of convent life, however, did not inhibit her cultivation of friendships within academic and court circles and allowed her time to read and study as well as to write hundreds of poems, and to compose liturgical sequences, comedies, and religious dramas.

The most fruitful period of her literary activity began in 1680 with the arrival of another vicereine, María Luisa Manrique de Lara y Gonzaga, marquise de la Laguna, countess of Paredes. The countess was nearly the same age as Sor Juana and had similar literary interests. She appreciated the nun's genius and was well connected in Madrid and Seville. It is undoubtedly through her efforts on her return to Spain in 1688 that three volumes of Sor Juana's works had been published by the time the nun died in 1695.

Sor Juana seems to have been on good terms with many highly placed ecclesiastical authorities, such as Archbishop and Viceroy (1673–80) Payo Enríque de Rivera and Mañuel Fernández de Santa Cruz, the bishop of Puebla. Her confessor in her late teens or early twenties as well as at the end of her life was the influential Jesuit and head of the Inquisition, Antonio Núñez de Miranda. Mexico City's most famous scholar, Carlos Sigüenza y Góngora, was a close friend, through whom apparently she kept abreast of scientific and philosophical developments in Europe. However, the obvious contradiction between her worldly contacts and interests and the pious ideal of a cloistered nun were a problem from the beginning. The arrival in 1682 of Francisco Aguiar y Seijas as archbishop of Mexico City—and thus Sor Juana's direct ecclesiastical superior—put a powerful voice among her detractors. Aguiar y Seijas was very conservative in his views of religious life, women's roles, and the frivolity of secular entertainments, such as those Sor Juana wrote, and of poetry contests, in which she participated.

The departure of the countess of Paredes for Spain six years later in 1688, though it strengthened Sor Juana's reputation abroad, left her in a more exposed political position at home. The publication of *Carta Athenagórica* (Letter Worthy of Athena) in 1690 seems to have been a turning point. This, her critique of a sermon of the Portuguese Jesuit, Antonio Vieira, published without her permission, was prefaced by an admonitory letter from the bishop of Puebla, which she then answered in her most famous work, the *Respuesta* (Response), an autobiographical defense of her intellectual integrity. It appears to have marked the beginning of a gradual end to her literary and scholarly activities.

THE NUN AND THE WORLD

SOR JUANA SCHOLARS are confronted with an abundance as well as a scarcity of material about her life. It is hard not to lament the disappearance of the hundreds of letters she wrote and the destruction of her convent's archives in the Mexican Revolution. On the other hand, the four volumes of her published writings reveal her interests, her style, and her genius. Numerous pieces written for official occasions raise interesting questions of a biographical nature regarding her relationship to the society of her day. There we find, among other things, some correspondence (in verse), a petition for clemency for a criminal, a celebration of victory over pirates, as well as a treatise on political power, *Allegorical Neptune*.

The major source for biographers to the present has been her own "intellectual autobiography," the *Response*, in which she traces her childhood, adolescence, entry into the convent, and her struggles there to continue her studies in the bustle of convent life and under pressure from outside forces. The other major source for Sor Juana's life is the biography written by the Spanish Jesuit Diego Calleja published in 1700 as part of the volume of her works *Fama y obras pósthumas* (Fame and posthumous works). Though Calleja never met Sor Juana, he had corresponded with her over many years, and was able to talk to people in Spain who knew her. It is obviously written by an enthusiastic supporter who is answering criticism directed toward her. Other near-contemporary reports are found in the biographies of the churchmen who were in contact with her: the bishop of Puebla, Fernández de Santa Cruz; the inquisitor Jesuit, Núñez de Miranda; and Archbishop Aguiar y Seijas. These, however, are stylized biographies of model ecclesiastics and tend to emphasize the extent to which they contributed to Sor Juana's "conversion" at the end of her life, rather than adding any substantially new information about her.

To present Sor Juana's life in some coherent fashion that goes beyond the sketch presented above means to move into the areas of contradiction and silence which frustrate and animate her biographers, and perhaps not coincidentally mirror the contradictions and silences which tantalize and tease in her works.

BIRTH AND CHILDHOOD

CLARITY ON SOR JUANA'S origins is muddled by three problems: a discrepancy about the year of her birth, controversy over her illegitimacy,[7] and the elusive identity of her father. Calleja, her first biographer, is very specific on the first matter: Madre Juana Inés was born on Thursday night, November 12, 1651 at eleven o'clock.[2] However, no trace of her baptismal record has been found in that year, though 1940s archival studies revealed an entry from December 2, 1648 of a child "Inés" designated as "daughter of the Church" (a euphemism for illegitimate) with godparents of the name "Ramírez."[3] I am aligning myself with most scholars (Paz et al.) who today accept the earlier date.[4]

The second problem is the issue of her illegitimacy. In both the Carmelite and the Hieronimite convent registers, Sor Juana refers to herself as "legitimate daughter of Don Pedro de Asbaje y Vargas Machuca and of Isabel Ramírez" (OC 4:522). Calleja twice emphasizes her legitimacy: "this fortunate Basque" *married* Doña Isabel Ramírez and "into this legitimate union" were born "other children."[5] However, in her will (1687) Isabel Ramírez declares that she has "remained a single woman" (*de estado soltera*) and that one of her "natural children" was Sor Juana.[6] In fact she had six "natural" children, three daughters—Sor Juana was the youngest—by Pedro Asbaje and three later by Diego Ruiz Lozano. What is behind this blatant contradiction? A necessary lie? Was Sor Juana's illegitimacy a dark secret known only to intimate family members? Editor Méndez Plancarte (1950), interprets her mother's will as part of a "death bed" confession in which she is anxious to "clear her record" before divine judgment of her "fault, in this case—felix culpa—which gave life to Sor Juana."[7]

Paz, on the other hand, explores Sor Juana's family tree as an example of a typical well-connected "middle class" family containing numerous long lasting illegitimate unions.[8] It would have hardly been possible, he maintains, to manage a pretense of legitimacy over decades in a climate variously described as extremely religious and extremely sensual[9] or of "extreme license" and "extreme prudery."[10] However if Sor Juana's illegitimacy were well known, why would she falsify a document? Is there a reason that has not yet been considered? One of the nun's epigrams has been interpreted to be a pained defense of her illegitimacy to a critic.[11]

> Not to be born of an honorable father
> would be a blemish, I must own,
> if receiving my being from no other
> I had not known it was his alone.

Far more generous was your mother
when she arranged your ancestry,
offering many a likely father
among whom to choose your pedigree.[12]

(OC 1:492)

Paz has been more discerning when he notes:

> Those who have commented on this epigram have not
> noticed that it refers not so much to her bastardy as to
> her father's origins. Was Asbaje not "honorable" because
> he was a plebeian or because he had committed some
> crime or misdeed?[13]

Indeed we are left with these questions unresolved.

Sor Juana's own account of her childhood in the *Response* which begins with a charming vignette of her first step into the world of books, indicates her precociousness. She describes herself tagging along behind her older sister who was sent for reading lessons to an *amiga* (as local teachers of young girls were known). When she saw what her sister was doing, she "felt the desire to learn to read burn within" her and she told the *amiga* that her mother also wanted her to take lessons. The teacher "did not believe because it was not believable," but included Juana in the lessons to please the girl. As it soon became obvious that Juana really was learning to read, both teacher and pupil hid the fact from her mother: the teacher because she wanted to get money for having taught both girls and Juana because she "thought they would beat me because I had done it without permission" (OC 4:445.215–34). By the time she was six or seven, she had also heard of the university and other schools in Mexico City. She began to pester her mother to let her wear men's clothes to go and study there.[14] Sor Juana comments that her mother "did not let me go and it was well that she would not." However, her thirst for books led her to read secretly the "many varied books" of her grandfather, "and no amount of punishment or scoldings could restrain" her (OC 4: 446.240–49).

Since the content of this library would reveal much about the background of her grandfather as well as early intellectual influences on Sor Juana, it is unfortunate that again we come up against a wall of silence and contradiction. According to the *Response*, her grandfather's library was the source of the astounding amount of *information* which she had acquired "at an age in which it appeared that I had hardly learned to speak" (OC 4:446.250–53). One book (an anthology of Latin poets) which belonged first to one Ramírez and then to Sor Juana was found in the 1930s. From notes in the margin, scholars deduce that this Ramírez was learned, married, and of "some social standing," and that he read the book between 1646 and 1652.[15] Calleja, on the other hand, writing in 1700, ten years after Sor Juana's autobiography and five years after her death, describes her grandfather's library as "a few books which she found in his house with no other purpose than to adorn a writing table," and adds, "a poverty under which she suffered for many years."[16] Calleja's de-emphasis of the learning of Sor Juana's grandfather may be seen as a manner of enhancing her own prodigious talent.

MEXICO CITY, THE COURT, AND THE CONVENT

FOR REASONS THAT are again unclear, Juana Inés Ramírez did move to Mexico City, possibly as early as 1656, and lived with her mother's sister María Ramírez and her husband, Juan de Mata, a wealthy merchant.[17] By that time, according to Calleja, she had already written her first *loa* (one-act play), which she composed for the feast of Corpus Christi because the prize offered was a book, and she "was always greedy for this sort of wealth."[18] In her *Response*, Sor Juana merely says that when she did come to Mexico City, people were astounded at her range of knowledge.

Upon the arrival of the marquis of Mancera and his wife, Leonor Carreto, in 1664, Juana Inés at age sixteen was introduced to the viceregal court. Here, she became exposed to the culture of court society which provided the basis for her romantic comedy, *Trials of a Noble House*, and countless poems for festive occasions, as well as her numerous love lyrics. She soon became a lady in waiting to the marquise who, according to Calleja, "could not live an instant without her Juana Inés."[19] She remained at court under her protection until 1667.

What was to be the future of this beautiful, talented, and extraordinarily intelligent girl? Calleja stresses her facility for poetry from an early age in a time when writing poetry was a major form of social entertainment.[20] Sor Juana in the *Response*, perhaps parodying her reputation, describes herself as "thinking in verse" and having to struggle to write prose. By 1668 her first poem had been

published. Her reputation for intellectual accomplishment was test-
ed at court when, at about seventeen, in a scene designed to imitate
the child Jesus disputing with the elders in the temple, she was
questioned by an assembly of forty scholars from all disciplines.
Calleja cites the marquis de Mancera, an eyewitness to the event:
"Like a Royal Galleon against canoes, she defended herself."[21]

Again in the *Response* an anecdote illuminates the life phase of
adolescence that includes awakening sexuality, higher education, and
the choice of a vocation. This complex Sor Juana treats in the space
of one paragraph: the first half describing her efforts to learn Latin;
the second her reasons for entering religious life. In the first bloom of
her youth, Juana Inés was so moved by enthusiasm for Latin that she
cut her hair four to six inches in order to motivate herself to greater
efforts. When she learned more slowly than her hair grew, she writes,
she would cut it again "because it did not seem right that a head
which was so bare of knowledge should be crowned with such an
adornment" (OC 4:446.265–67). The implication was, of course,
that knowledge was a more fitting adornment for the head, even a
woman's head, than beautiful hair. Her choice of words reminds of a
Pauline text: (1 Cor 11:14–15) "Does not nature herself teach you
that while long hair disgraces a man, it is a woman's glory." Even as
an adolescent, she is willing to sacrifice this "crown" for that of learning. Antonio Alatorre has questioned the "historical nature" of the
hair-cutting because of his dating her twenty Latin lessons "during
those few months" before she entered the Carmelite convent from
which she later withdrew because of illness.[22] Indeed given that normal hair growth is one-half inch a month, it is unlikely that Sor Juana
would really have been able to cut her hair four to six inches several
times during the period she learned her *grammatica*. Furthermore
the repeated emphasis on her "slow wittedness," when she has just
described the astonishment of the sophisticates in Mexico City at the
cleverness and prodigious memory in one who "had hardly had time
to learn to speak" (OC 4:446.252–53), also suggests the incident's
fictional nature. Why would a young woman who as a girl has been
described as a prodigious learner, have tremendous difficulty with
Latin? Furthermore the reported witness of her Latin tutor, Martin
de Olivas, stresses that cutting her hair "a bit" once was enough to
stimulate her memory. All these suggest that the symbolic construction of the incident with its Pauline subtext is what is of primary
importance for the nun.

Immediately following her narration of this anecdote, Sor
Juana writes, "I became a nun because although I knew that this
state of life had many incidental aspects that were repugnant to me,
though not the central ones, considering everything, given my total
lack of desire for marriage, it seemed the least inappropriate and the
most decent way to secure my salvation" (OC 4:446.268–73). This
sudden conflation of two seemingly unrelated matters is often a sign
in Sor Juana's prose that a second level of meaning is intended.
Indeed the passage is reminiscent of another text often cited in
defining the role of women which refers to the custom of women
who pray and prophesy in the community doing so with covered
heads. "A woman brings shame on her head if she prays or prophe-
sies bareheaded; it is as bad as if her head were shaved. If a woman
does not cover her head she might as well have her hair cut off; but
if it is a disgrace for her to be cropped and shaved, then she should
cover her head" (1 Cor 11:4–6). Juana Inés cropped her own
"unveiled head" before entering the convent for the sake of knowledge, much as students were tonsured as part of their official entry
into the university. Her state of cropped hair for wisdom's sake was
not "the most decent" state, the nun maintains (OC 4:446.273).
This corresponds to Paul's judgment of the unveiled woman: "it is
as bad as if her head were shaved." Entering the convent would
require having her head shaved, but would cover it with a veil, making what would otherwise appear indecent acceptable.[23]

Though a reasonable marriage was not inconceivable without
dowry or name, her future at court was precarious. Looking back
on her motivation twenty years later, Sor Juana writes that the convent was "the least inappropriate and the most decent" way for her
to live. She describes her hesitation to enter a state of life which she
found "repugnant" in its accidental aspects though not in its essen-
tials. Given her "total disinclination (*negación*) to marriage"(OC
4:446.271–72)[24] she maintains she would have preferred living
alone with her books, without the demands community life would
impose, but unnamed "learned people" convinced her that convent
life would be the best means of securing her salvation. Though it
was common for both men and women to enter religious life for
economic and familial reasons, it is rare, perhaps unique, to find
such a sober, rational assessment of entry into religious life in a text
such as Sor Juana's *Response,* which is an apology and a defense of
her life as an intellectual.

If Sor Juana's motivation for becoming a nun is equivocal and opaque, she has left no record at all of her reasons for leaving the Reformed Carmelite convent of San José in November of 1667, after three months, thereby creating another empty space for the conjecture of biographers. Juan de Oviedo, the biographer of Sor Juana's sometime confessor, Antonio Núñez de Miranda, S.J., credits Núñez with securing her entry into both the Carmelite and later the Hieronimite convents. He maintains that she left because of reasons of health, doctors ascertaining that her constitution could not survive the rigors of the strict observance of the Carmelites.[25] However, since in a recently (1980) discovered communication of Sor Juana (the "Monterrey Letter") to her confessor Núñez, she chides him for publicly claiming credit for her taking up religious life, Núñez's own biographer is hardly a reliable source in this matter.[26] Others assume that the strict discipline of the Carmelites was not to her liking.[27] Sabat de Rivers mentions that this convent admitted "very few Criollos" (Hispanic women born in Mexico rather than Spain), suggesting Sor Juana might not have fit in because of the assumed superiority of the Spanish born.[28]

EARLY ECCLESIASTICAL CONNECTIONS: ARCHBISHOP AND VICEROY FRAY PAYO ENRIQUE DE RIVERA

SOR JUANA'S MOVE from the court to the convent allowed her to continue to study and be able to accept commissions to write because they enhanced the reputation of her convent. Furthermore, good relations with the viceroys were always an advantage in the event that favors were needed. An example of the support she enjoyed as well as her own self-confidence and spirit of fun is illustrated in her relationship with Viceroy and Archbishop Fray Payo Enríque de Rivera.[29]

Appointed archbishop in 1668, he arrived in Mexico City the year preceding Sor Juana's entry into the Hieronimite convent. A native of Seville, he was a son (possibly a "natural son")[30] of the duke of Alcalá, viceroy of Naples. His family was one of the wealthiest in Spain.[31] Fray Payo had come to New Spain in 1657 when he was named bishop of Guatemala. While in Guatemala he had used his influence to support the establishment of the first religious order in America, the Bethlehemites, and he encouraged their expansion to Mexico City where they established a hospital and primary schools.[32] He was a poet as well as a religious writer and participated in poetry tournaments and collaborated on the construction of a triumphal arch to welcome the new viceroy, the duke of Veraguas in 1673. He is a remarkable figure in Sor Juana's life, if only because he is the single highly placed churchman mentioned by name in her published works. Two poems refer to him and two address him directly. One sonnet praises Brother Diego de Rivera as cantor of the works of the "arzobispo Virrey Don Fray Payo Enríquez de Ribera" (OC 1:307–8). Another poem celebrates a scholar for applauding a book written by Don Payo (OC 1:248–49). Another which addresses Rivera as "simple sacred shepherd," commends him as the author of a treatise (since lost) on the doctrine of the Immaculate Conception, also a favorite subject of Sor Juana (OC 1:19).

The most elaborate poem, a "romance," requests that the bishop administer the sacrament of confirmation to Sor Juana (OC 1:32–40). Its light manner suggests intimacy, and a complex series of references presupposes a density of shared culture both intellectual and literary, local and universal. The expected references to classical antiquity, bits of ecclesiastical gossip, and pointed references to contemporary poets and playwrights from Spain and Mexico attest to the nun's familiarity with contemporary literature[33] as well as Enríquez de Rivera's literary interests. The third section of the poem contains her actual request to be confirmed (OC 1:38), revealing in the process the lengthy delay often involved in the appointment of bishops in New Spain and the receipt of their faculties. This leaves so many Mexicans "unconfirmed," Sor Juana comments, that they are left no recourse than to try to "confirm themselves" in the faith. In the final section (OC 1:38), after alluding to the rumor that Rivera had been elected cardinal archbishop of Seville, she imagines him becoming pope and setting her free with the keys of St. Peter (only the pope could release her from enclosure), so she could come and visit him in Rome.

A number of aspects of the poem suggest that the actual meaning of the poem lies elsewhere than in its proclaimed intent. The bantering, intimate tone suggests a relationship of easy familiarity which belies a serious "formal request." Though ostensibly about wanting to receive the sacrament of confirmation, it is atypical in its presentation of that sacrament. Confirmation which is associated especially with the affirming of the baptismal faith of the believers through the Holy Spirit, and which opens up their full participation in the life of the Church, is administered by anointing with chrism or holy oils. Recipients were encouraged to become "soldiers of Christ" and were given a symbolic slap on the cheek to symbolize their willingness to suffer for the faith. Sor Juana's only reference to the "theology" of the sacrament of confirmation is to the "slap": "I humbly beg you to lay your hand upon me, seeing that I need it. Give me a slap (*bofetón*) . . . that will resonate in my soul with the grace of its sound" (OC 1:37). References to other sacraments are hardly more reverential. "Last rites" or extreme unction is described in terms of the fright it gives people, since it was an indication that they were considered near death. Her reception of the Eucharist "the body of the Holy Sacrifice" is God's primary reason for sparing her. Baptism is mentioned as part of her complaint of not being confirmed: "See, so strong is my feeling about not having confirmation that I'm considering 'un-baptizing' myself" (*peinso que me "desbautizo"*), (OC 1:37). Even the Trinity does not escape Sor Juana's spirit of levity, when in the final formulation of her three-part request for confirmation she writes: "Give me, in the name of the one God, / the sacrament I ask of you / and if you won't do it for the One / give it to me for the Three in One (*Por Uno y Trino*)" (OC 1:37).

There is some internal evidence that the motivation for the poem is a near brush with "literary death" through a threat from the Inquisition, rather than physical death. Sensing another purpose behind mention of a bout with typhoid, ostensibly the motivation for her petitioning confirmation, Paz sees the illness as "an excuse for the rhetorical games and playfulness which characterize much of the poem."[34] It is an example of Sor Juana's "baroque abstraction" which converts actual experience into "erudition and burlesque poetry." Another interpretation emerges if attention is paid to the numerous expressions which have double meanings connected with printing and publishing, especially in the final fifteen verses of the poem, leaving open the possibility that the "near brush with death" is meant as an allusion to "literary death." There she thanks Enríque de Rivera for the "licenses" he had given, which she compares to divine favors, and for which she is giving him "these writings . . . written in her own blood" to "his heart for their archives." Méndez Plancarte speculates that the licenses were permissions to receive visitors during her illness, but if the "illness" near death, is a crisis in her writing career, they may be the licenses to publish. The "archives of the heart" of the bishop may be the place where her "writings" are safe from another archive, that of the Inquisition. In the last stanza the "crosses of the office," obviously a play on words with her own name "Cruz," have been interpreted as the burdens of Enríquez de Rivera's episcopal office. They have a different meaning if *oficio* is read "Santo Oficio," Holy Office, or Inquisition. The "crosses," correspondingly, might be the passages crossed out by the Inquisition.

In 1680 Rivera was replaced as viceroy by Tomás Antonio de la Cerda. The new viceroy's wife María Luisa, countess of Paredes, was a cousin of Rivera and would become in her turn a powerful patroness and close friend of the nun.

2

God among the Nations

Sweet Songbird of Mexico, swan
whose voice if heard by the Stygian lake
a second time would return Eurydice to you,
a second time the Dolphin would be rendered human.

Sor Juana to Sigüenza y Góngora (OC 1:308–9)

ART OF THE fascination that Sor Juana exercised over her Spanish readers was due to the fact that they regarded her as Mexican, from the "New World," even as "Indian." The engraving of her portrait in the volume of her posthumous works configures her as a bridge between a Spanish conquistador and an Indian warrior. For her part, Sor Juana as Mexican was keenly aware of the complexities of the intermingling of cultures in the New World, and of the effects this had on the missionary efforts of the Spaniards as they moved into the culture of the multitude of peoples lumped together as Indios. Though she does not state them explicitly, her views can be seen "at work" in many ways.

CONSTRUCTION OF THE TRIUMPHAL ARCH

THE NUN'S FIRST major commission, to compose an allegory for the triumphal arch welcoming the new viceroy, Tomás Antonio de la Cerda, gave her the opportunity to come to grips with the more general issue of the mingling of cultures. She could also at least begin to address some of the wider problems involved in the evangelization process. These included the relationship of non-Christian religions to Christianity, the nature of revelation, and the manner of God's indwelling in non-Christian religions. Sor Juana returns to the great missionaries and ethnographers of the sixteenth century as a source of her arguments.

The commission, accompanied by a substantial monetary award for Sor Juana's convent, was a high honor. It was part of the pageantry accompanying a change of office either of the viceroy or the bishop. The arch, a wooden structure much like a stage set, was erected and covered with canvas. On it, various scenes were painted to correspond to the allegory developed by the author. A poem explaining the meaning of the paintings was to be read, perhaps even sung at the ceremony. A book length description of the paintings on the arch, as well as scholarly explanation of the deeper significance of the allegory, would be published.

Since a second triumphal arch designed to welcome the viceroy to the city was executed by the eminent scholar, Sigüenza y Góngora, Sor Juana was paired with the other acknowledged scholar as the best the city had to offer, occurred in 1680, when she would have been in her early thirties. Sigüenza included lavish praise of Sor Juana in his description of his arch. He acclaimed her "sublime erudition" as being of encyclopedic range and universal scope "giving Mexico the honor of having in one unique individual a capacity for knowledge and wisdom equal to that of all the learned women of the past."[1] A priest and mathematician, Sigüenza was unusual in his contact with and advocacy of indigenous cultures. He was known to have made extensive studies of Indian customs, and even suffered near financial ruin because of his defense of the inheritance of an Indian prince.

Both Mexican authors were concerned with bringing to expression a group that was silenced: the indigenous populations of Mexico. However, references to the Aztec heritage are veiled in Sor Juana's allegory, in contrast to the explicit Aztec imagery used by her friend Sigüenza y Góngora. The examples of virtuous kings he uses for his "mirror of princes" are Aztec Gods. As "love of the native land" inspires people to venerate their own great heroes, so the Aztecs venerated their heroic kings as "gods," a practice for which he finds support in the Christian tradition of honoring princes as "images of God."[2] He clearly sees his cultural ancestors as including the Aztecs, and presumes that the viceroy will not take offense if he, like the Austrian house of Hapsburg, brings the history of *his* birthplace into that of the Spanish monarchy. He even suggests that the viceroy become an advocate of this history.[3]

Though the lament for a lost culture can be heard out of the text of *Allegorical Neptune*, Sor Juana's allegory is more subtle. Basically, whereas Sigüenza uses the Aztec pantheon, she uses the classical Greco-Roman religious system as an analogue to the Aztec one. For the early missionaries and historians of Mexico, the Greco-Roman pantheon had functioned as a translating tool, both for their understanding the Aztec religious system and for their introducing it to a European audience. The parallels that such authors as Durán, Motolinía, and others established became part of the more general discussion of the nature of the religious belief of the "New World" natives. Were their "gods" demons that the devil had set up to lead them astray from the one true God who is revealed in creation? Or were these gods inadequate attempts to represent the one true God, needing only an appropriate "translation" through Christian missionary activity?

Sor Juana's reserve needs to be seen against the background of the sixteenth-century debate on the question of the humanity of the Indians and the Church's responsibility to them.[4] Over a century before (1550–51), at the court of Phillip II, the renowned Renaissance scholar, Juan Ginés de Sepúlveda, proponent of Aristotle's idea of natural slavery, and Bartolomé de Las Casas, defender of the Indians, debated the idea of the oneness of "all humanity" without resolving the question. As early as 1577,[5] in a reversal of policy, the Spanish crown suspended the dissemination of the works of the great chroniclers of Aztec customs; Franciscans: Sahagún, Mendieta, Motolinía, and Dominicans Diego Durán and Las Casas.[6]

Sigüenza, for all his admiration of the nun at one point, seems to be criticizing her because she has recourse to a "foreign pantheon" rather than the Mexican (Aztec) one as the basis for her allegory. However, her caution was probably well founded: her works were published and Sigüenza's ethnographic studies were not, and as a result, except for a few quotations, are lost to us.

* * *

SOR JUANA'S MONUMENT

SOR JUANA'S FIRST major publication, *Allegorical Neptune,* remained her longest work, and was fully representative of her later thought. Expectations of the work were practical as well as aesthetic. Praise of the marquis was expected to be linked with advocacy for the needs of his subjects.[7] Both Sor Juana and Sigüenza mention the recurrent flooding that devastated Mexico City, and in a mix of mythology and contemporary history request the building or repairing of dikes.[8] In the third panel, Sor Juana depicts Neptune using his trident to stabilize the floating island of Delos (painted to resemble the city of Mexico). Latona, who is pregnant by Jupiter with Apollo (god of the sun) and Diana (goddess of the moon), flees to escape the wrath of the offended wife Juno. Mexican readers would associate the Roman divinities of sun and moon as references to the great Aztec pyramids of the sun and moon in Teotihuacán. She writes that this island (Delos/Mexico City) seems to become the entire "new world," which was hidden for many centuries under water, and only discovered by the grace of Neptune (here, obviously the Spanish) who crossed the ocean to enjoy its immense riches. The eighth panel depicts "el magnífico Templo Mejicano," the cathedral, but less apparently also the Aztec *templo mayor* which had been razed for the construction of the cathedral. Opposite this panel, Sor Juana places the great defeated city of antiquity, Troy, whose walls were said to have been built by Neptune, again suggesting the presence of the defeated culture beneath that of the conquerors, represented by the viceroy.

MIRROR OF PRINCES: CRITIQUE OF THE IDOLATRY OF POWER

SOR JUANA, AS AUTHOR of the arch, is called upon to do more than ask for favors of the ruler. She is expected to develop a "mirror of princes" or a treatise on the virtues of the ideal ruler. In this connection, the nun explores the relationship of secular to spiritual power. The ideal ruler would not aspire to divine power, though he might seem to have godlike virtues and talents. She uses Natal Conti's theory that the gods of antiquity were originally excellent princes, who, either because of their rare virtues or because of their inventions, had divinity attributed to them. As a result, it is not because Neptune *created* the bull that it is associated with him (in the Christian sense of "creation"), but because the bull was a symbol of wisdom and Neptune was originally a man renowned for his wisdom (OC 4:368). The underlying implication of this rationalizing of ancient divinities is that even the most exalted comparison of the ruler can never make him "divine." Even metaphorically, the ruler does not have the right to be compared to the divinity because of his office, but only because of what is godlike in his virtues and talents. Sigüenza y Góngora, in his companion arch, voices similar concerns: "the power of governments is 'godlike' to the extent it imitates God's divine goodness in its works."[9]

In Sor Juana's "mirror of princes," wisdom is the virtue which is indispensable for the monarch. All virtues are interconnected, but wisdom is the "root and source from which emanate all the others" (OC 4:367.364). The republic cannot survive without a wise leader "because it is wisdom and not gold" which is the real crown of princes (OC 4:367.368). She proceeds to define the other virtues of the viceroy as related to wisdom: His piety is manifest through judgment which sees only the merits of the case, and is not influenced by revenge of offended honor (OC 4:381). He is the defender of learning (382–85) and prudent in judgment (385–88). He lets reason govern the state (389–92), and is even described as the "father of giant thoughts" (396). Finally, and above all, he asks God for wisdom in governing (398).

FEMININE WISDOM

IF WISDOM IS the source of good government, the source of wisdom is feminine. Neptune is dependent on, one could almost say, the creature of a woman: the goddess Isis. As Neptune's mother she would have impressed him with the value of wisdom (OC 4:363.364). Considering that Sor Juana's discussion of the origins and interrelationships of Isis and other goddesses associated with wisdom continues in different variations for over two hundred lines, *Allegorical Neptune* provides early evidence of Sor Juana's feminist concerns.[10] Again following Natal Conti, Isis, Egyptian goddess of fertility and wisdom, was originally a celebrated queen praised for her wisdom by Plato, Plutarch, and other ancient writers. Insisting on the feminine source of wisdom, the nun rejects the opinion of Jacob Bolduc who developed the origin of the word *Isis* through an etymology of *is* (Hebrew for man) tracing the wisdom of Egypt back to two men (*Is-is*), Misrain and Heber (Gen. 10), rather than to the woman, Isis.

Egypt is not the only civilization to see wisdom in female guise. Again Sor Juana uses Greco-Roman culture as a base. She draws one of the scenes on the arch to portray Athena/Minerva, as she vanquishes Neptune in a contest for the honor of the city of Athens. She transforms this "defeat" into "victory" for Neptune by insisting that "Minerva/Athena" represents his reason. By letting himself be conquered by his rational faculties (OC 4:388.392), he demonstrated his wisdom.[11]

AMBIVALENT TITLES

SOR JUANA DOES not neglect the expected flattery of the monarch. Portraits of the marquis and marquise are inserted over faces of Neptune and his wife Amphitrite as they stand in a chariot skimming over the waves. Despite the intended compliment of the arch's general conception, it becomes obvious that the comparison of the marquis with Neptune was suggested not so much by a similarity of character and qualities as by the happy associations afforded in his long list of names, titles, and offices. Like Neptune, son of royal Saturn, the marquis is "son of Spain's royal line"(OC 4:369). Like Neptune, whose mother (Isis) is wisdom, he is descended from el "Señor Rey Don Alonso, el Sabio" (King Alfonso the Wise). Like Neptune, he is the brother of Jupiter, the god of the skies. The marquis's brother, the duke of Medina *Coeli* (sky) had been appointed prime minister to Charles II the previous February. His title, "Marquis de la Laguna" (lagoon), ties him to Neptune's watery world. As count *de Paredes* (walls), he is connected to Neptune who built the walls of Troy (OC 4:369–70). Through an elaborate etymology of the word "marquis," Sor Juana associates the viceroy with Neptune as tamer of horses, so that he becomes "Prefect and Lord of the Cavalry and of the equestrian arts." His surname, "Mañuel de la *Cerda*" (hair of a horses tail or mane), reinforces the connection (OC 4:370) and incidentally moves the comparison from the tamer of horses to the horse itself. Sor Juana alludes to a story (OC 4:370.495), which Sigüenza elaborates in his description of his arch, that one of the sons of Alonso el Sabio was born with a long braid down his back (thus the family name, Cerda). The nun interprets this ancestral trait as a sign from God that the marquis was destined to be a commander of cavalry.

ISSUES OF CENSORSHIP

SOR JUANA WAS aware of her precarious position as a woman author of the arch, who by constructing a "mirror of princes" in effect was instructing the monarch through his official representative, the viceroy. Her awareness of her delicate situation as a woman emerges in the elaborate, multilayered introduction to her description of the arch. Her hesitation to accept the commission, she explains, is based on her conviction that her meager talent cannot hope to describe the exalted person of the marquis. She presumes the cathedral chapter has selected her on the general principle that they, like God, choose to work through a weak instrument. Moreover, whereas the eloquence of learned men might be intimidating, a woman's "gentle ignorance" would be more likely to inspire the viceroy to grant the favors which the chapter would undoubtedly seek. The churchmen, she maintains, by selecting her have followed the example of Joab, King David's general, who sends the woman, Tekoa, to present his case to the king (2 Sam 14:1–20). Like Tekoa, Sor Juana speaks not of her own volition, but at the request of higher authorities (OC 4:358).

The second reason the nun gives for her reluctance to agree to the task of writing is fear of her readers' criticism. Even Cicero, she maintains, "sought mediocrity of expression" because he feared the envy of his readers (OC 4:357). At this point Sor Juana uses the convention of affected modesty also as camouflage for a subtext critiquing censorship. Her classically educated audience would know that Cicero, the greatest Roman orator, was executed, his head and hands displayed in the Senate chamber, after a remark about the young emperor Augustus: "The young man should be given praise, distinctions and then be disposed of."[12] In the poem read at the ceremony itself, she describes the arch as "Cicero without a tongue" and as "a mute Demosthenes." Obviously the surface meaning of the trope is that the arch speaks eloquently in pictures and symbols without words, but both these orators met with tragic ends because of their outspoken opposition to the rule of tyrannical emperors, Cicero against Augustus and Demosthenes against Alexander the Great.

The oppression involved in speaking in a restrictive society emerges again when the nun makes an explitic reference to silence. She begs to "venture a guess" of her own as to why Neptune is regarded as the god of silence (OC 4:361). The Egyptians, she maintains, used the fish, as a symbol of silence. Neptune's subjects, the fish are the only creatures without a voice: "only the fish among all creatures is mute" (OC 4:361). Twice—once in Spanish and once in Latin—Sor Juana reminds her audience of the story of Rhadamanthus, judge of the kingdom of the dead and founder of laws who "changed the loquacious into fish, so that those who had erred by speaking too much should make up for it by eternal silence" (OC 4:361). In this manner, Sor Juana is able to appear to exalt the viceroy, who rules over obedient subjects, while simultaneously intimating his subjects have good reason to fear speaking openly.[13]

The darker note struck by this subtext may be a reflection of opposition the nun had encountered because of the commission. The controversy surrounding Sor Juana's arch may have been one of the reasons her friend Sigüenza y Góngora included such high praise of her in his own "arch" (*Theatro de Virtudes Politicas*) as a way of countering malicious gossip. In fact, this extended praise of her intellectual abilities follows a passage in which he endeavors to deflect some of the criticism his work will encounter, using expressions such as, "Not everyone admires and loves the same thing."[14] He ends his self-defense with a nearly caustic proscription (citing an authority, Pope Adrian): "Whosoever publicly invents writings or words injurious to the fame of others, and has manifestly not proven what they write shall be flogged."[15] The first thing that comes to mind is, of course, that Sigüenza himself has had to suffer such abuses, but since the next chapter begins with high praise of Sor Juana and a defense of her work, his comment may be a reference to some of the gossip stirred up against her.

In fact the commission to construct the triumphal arch was a mixed blessing, as Sor Juana reveals in a 1682 letter to Antonio Núñez de Miranda, her confessor. Núñez had been with her since her days as lady in waiting to the marquise of Mancera. As censor for the Inquisition, and prefect of the Congregation of the Most Pure Conception of the Virgin Mary, a religious association of high-ranking officials and nobility, he had powerful connections to the elite.[16] Deeply involved in the spiritual direction of nuns, he wrote numerous descriptions on their ideal and not so ideal behaviors. One of the first of these was a pamphlet railing against the worldly relations of nuns with their pious admirers in the convent parlors. There he insisted on a most rigorous type of obedience to the spiritual director whose "light was the light of heaven" guiding his "daughters" on the treacherous paths of this life. Furthermore, each nun was to keep the spiritual director designated—the "one, unique, invariable . . . consulted, believed, and followed as a heavenly oracle."[17] Núñez also denounced the reading of profane books, comedies, novels, and the theater in general. This last tendency especially had led several scholars to speculate that the strict ascetic Núñez had broken with Sor Juana between 1682 and 1692, the period of her most intense literary activity.[18] The "Monterrey letter" also called "spiritual self-defense" reveals the contrary: it was Sor Juana who dismissed the Jesuit.

Núñez's displeasure seems to have reached a fever pitch because of her construction of the triumphal arch. *The Letter of Monterrey* reveals Sor Juana's indignation at the campaign of slander which he had been waging against her. She writes with irony of "her unforgivable fault" of having acceded to the repeated requests of the cathedral chapter in the name of the archbishop and her superior. In a passionate outburst she continues,

> Now it would be my wish that Your Reverence, with all the clarity of your judgment, put yourself in my place and consider what you would have replied in this situation. Would you answer that you could not? That would have been a lie. That you did not wish to? That would have been disobedience. That you did not know how? They did not ask more than I knew. That the vote was badly taken? That would have been impudent audacity, vile and gross ingratitude to those who honored me by believing that an ignorant woman knew how to do what such brilliant minds solicited. So I had no choice but to obey.[19]

At the same time, she gives a more general picture of the persecution she suffers because of the unsought notoriety which her God-given talent has caused her:

> Of what envy am I not the target? of what malice am I not the object? What actions do I take without fear? What word do I speak without misgiving? Women feel that men surpass them, and that I seem to place myself on a level with men; some wish that I did not know so much; others say that I ought to know more to merit such applause; elderly women do not wish that other women know more than they; young women, that others present a good appearance; and one and all wish me to

> conform to the rules of their judgment; so that from all
> sides comes such a singular martyrdom as I deem none
> other has ever experienced.[20]

Even her penmanship her convent sisters found too masculine and they insisted that she change it to conform to their ideal.

Furthermore, this text substantiates Sor Juana's consciousness of her independence as a woman, an intellectual, and as a lay person.[21] She takes Núñez to task for claiming he would have had her married had he known she would write verses in the convent. She reminds him that arrangements for her convent dowry had been made without him, that she had only known him a short time when she entered the convent. Most importantly she denies that he had "authority to dispose of my person and the free will God granted me."[22] By nature she is "not as humbled as other daughters" and is "sorely tried" by his abuse.[23] As an intellectual she informs him of the many canonized women and men who have written poetry or been interested in literature and of the acknowledged virtues of pagan philosophers. "That St. Anthony was saved in his holy ignorance is well and good. St. Augustine chose the other path, and neither of them went astray."[24] As a lay person, she suggests that she is not under obligation to have a spiritual director. "I shall therefore be able to govern myself by the general rules of the Holy Mother Church, until God enlightens me to do otherwise, and choose freely the spiritual father that I wish."[25] She strives to attain salvation not sanctity, which cannot be commanded. "Only God's grace and assistance can make a saint."[26] Thus, it is clear that even her earliest work aroused controversy. Núñez, displeased with her refusal to conform to his view of the ideal nun, could through his connections, seriously damage her reputation. However despite this, she was able to break with him, taking another confessor, Pedro de Arellano y Sossa, one of Núñez's "spiritual sons."[27]

Sor Juana did not allow Núñez de Miranda's opposition to rein in her creative powers and eight years later she sent the manuscript for the first volume of her collected works, *Inundación Castálida*, back to Spain with the countess of Paredes.

3

⊱✵⊰

Comedies to the Honor and Glory of Bread[1]

Noble Mexicans
whose ancient line
has its source
in the radiance
of the sun,
Since today is
the blessed day
in which we consecrate
our greatest relic . . .
let devotion
be joined with gladness
and in festive splendor
let us celebrate
the great God of the Seeds.

(OC 3:3–4)

SOR JUANA'S THREE sacramental dramas, *The Martyr of the Sacrament: Saint Hermenegild*, *The Scepter of Joseph*, and *The Divine Narcissus*, with their *loas* (one-act preface plays), are placed together as *comicos sacras* (sacred comedies) in the 1692 Seville edition of volume two of her works. In addition to the theme of the Eucharist all three plays (which appeared together in 1692, the bicentennial of the first Columbus voyage) are associated with the pre-Christian Americas, through their *loas*. They contain a more explicit development of themes only hinted at or tentatively explored in *Allegorical Neptune*. Indeed, in the first of these, prefacing *The Martyr of the Sacrament*, Columbus himself makes an appearance as he returns to Spain after his first voyage. He rushes into the play in progress, where theology students of Sor Juana's day are debating the greatest benefits of Christ's love. Only partially aware of the magnitude of his discovery, he already knows with certainty that he has toppled the limits of the "old World" symbolized by the "pillars of Hercules." In the *loa* to *The Scepter of Joseph*, a partially catechized Idolatry again interrupts the debating theologians, Faith, Nature, Law of Grace, Law of Nature, who have just been congratulating themselves on their success at the conversion of the Indies. Idolatry, enraged and baffled, objects that she cannot even enter the conversation because she does not share sufficient communality of "language." In the *loa* to *The Divine Narcissus*, the pagans of America appear celebrating their "great God of the Seeds," as quoted above, only to have their celebration interrupted by the arrival of the Spanish conquistador and his partner Religion.

Drama of the Eucharist

The publication of these dramas and their *loas*, thanks to the patronage of the countess of Paredes, allowed Sor Juana's ideas access to one of the most powerful and public means of expression in her time: the stage. Indeed, Calderón de la Barca, arguably the greatest dramatist of the Golden Age, stressed their power as theological teaching, calling them: "sermons put in verse in which ideas are dramatized and questions of Sacred Theology are presented which the mind can neither explain nor comprehend."[2] All three of the one-act plays with which Sor Juana prefaces her sacramental dramas are designed to point up the limits of the "discussion of the schools" in theological debate and to plead gracefully for drama as a more appropriate form for the communication of theological truths than rational discourse because of the very nature of "divine things." Again, Calderón de la Barca expresses the sensitivity of the age to the power, as well as the limits, of dramatic representations when he describes all forms as inadequate, even "indecent" as to their capacity for representing the divine. Drama, however, he adds, in as far as it uses the human form, the image of God, is the most appropriate vehicle to represent the divine form and action.[3] Sor

Juana clearly follows this line: The arts are at least as appropriate a vehicle for exploration of divine truth and for teaching it to others as discursive theology.

Intended to be performed for the feast of Corpus Christi, the *autos sacramentales* celebrated the mystery of the transformation of bread and wine into Body and Blood of Jesus. Though this had been an important feast before the Reformation, in the face of the Reformers' differences with Catholicism on the nature of the real presence of Christ in the Eucharist,[4] it had become a corporate celebration of the most important of sacred mysteries, a bodily manifestation of spiritual truths in plays, pageants, and processions of the corporate body of Christ, the Church. These all came together on this feast, when the eucharistic wafer enshrined in the monstrance like the center of a sun was carried in solemn procession through the streets of cities, towns, and villages of Catholic Europe and its far-flung colonies. Preceding and following it were representatives of all religious orders, confederations, guilds, and floats that were like stages upon which the plays were performed. This conscious fusing of art and theology in the sacramental dramas was also seen as (again Calderón) "a dance of jubilation against heretical arguments" in which each bell on the dancers' dress was a "syllogism against the infidel apostate."[5]

Yet to consider the Eucharist as merely limited to the teaching of the "real Presence" of Christ in the elements of bread and wine is to ignore the symbolic density that is concentrated in the sacrament.[6] In as far as Jesus was a moral example for his followers, his supreme act of love and sacrifice was a model for them to follow in their lives, calling forth love and sacrifice for others. In as far as Jesus was seen as doing the will of his Father, he was a model of obedience to divine providence. The crucifix laden with the naked body of Christ, as opposed to the simpler Protestant cross stripped of the body, was also a central part of the visual experience of celebration of the Eucharist. The image of the altar, suggesting the sacrificial cult of the Old Testament was doubled by that of the "altar of the Cross" on which Christ "our pascal sacrifice" was offered. Even when the suffering body was contorted and streaming with blood it symbolized the reality of the resurrection of that body. Each of Sor Juana's sacramental dramas is about different aspects of the Eucharist. Hermenegild, in his person, represents the effects of the "fruit" of Eucharist. He overcomes the conflicting demands of the virtues, and incarnates love which is the virtue most central to the Eucharist. *The Scepter of Joseph* emphasizes bread as needed to feed the physically and spiritually hungry, as well as pointing up the mysteriousness of God's working in history. *The Divine Narcissus* centers on the meaning of Christ's sacrificial death as historical basis for the Eucharist.

The celebration of the Eucharist in its two central dimensions, that of meal and sacrifice contains within it two of the basic aspects of all religions: that of nourishment and deprivation, giving life and giving up life, living and dying. At the same time it is historically anchored in the person of Jesus, in his commemorative meal with his disciples and in his sacrificial death on the cross. This historical connection expands backward in time into the history of the chosen people of God, the Israelites, the people from whom Jesus came, and forward into the history of the new people of God, inheritors of the Kingdom of Israel, the people who saw themselves as coming from Jesus, and forming a new community, of those called out, *ekklesia* or the Church.

When considered in terms of their order within the 1692 Seville volume, the three *autos* demonstrate a reverse chronology. We see a shift in the frame of the theological discourse from one of inter-Christian controversy in *The Martyr of the Sacrament: St. Hermenegild* to the Old Testament, and consequently, Hebrew/Jewish prefiguring of eucharistic truths in *The Scepter of Joseph,* to a third level of the presence of religious truths in pagan, non-Christian dress in *The Divine Narcissus,* suggesting the *anima naturaliter christiana,* which was part of Jesuit missionary theology. Hermenegild can be aware of the full meaning of the sacrament, albeit in faith. The story of Joseph can prefigure the truths of the Eucharist, but these are only manifest from a "future perspective" (prophecy). Joseph himself is not aware of their symbolic significance. Pagan myth, such as that of Narcissus, and by implication that of the pre-Christian Americas can also anticipate, though darkly, Christian truths.

THE MARTYR OF THE SACRAMENT

HERMENEGILD (d. 585) WAS the eldest son of the Visigoth King Leovigild of Spain, who, as an Arian Christian, believed that the Son of God was "the first creature" from which the creation of all others flowed, rather than, as the orthodox professed, as existing "before all ages" and equal, not subordinate to the Father. Subsequent to Hermenegild's marriage to the orthodox Christian Ingund, and through the efforts of the Catholic bishop Leander, he converted to Catholicism, causing a rift with his father which grew into open warfare. In order to obtain financial and military aid from the Eastern Christians, he was forced to turn over his wife and son to the Greek emperor as security. After a disastrous battle with his father's forces, he was captured. His forgivness for his insurrection was made conditional on his receiving communion from the hand of the Arian bishop at Easter. When he refused, he was immediately executed. Hermenegild was martyred in 585. His biography was written by Pope Gregory VII, who was a great friend of Leander, the bishop of Seville responsible for Hermenegild's conversion.[7] Nonetheless it was only due to the efforts of King Phillip II of Spain that in 1585, a thousand years later, his cult was authorized in Spain. Sor Juana's play about St. Hermenegild is the only one among the thousands in print to feature the Gothic saint as hero of a sacramental drama.[8]

Hermenegild's martyrdom, for the sake of "the correct understanding of the Eucharist," made him an ideal model for a post-Reformation Church that saw as one of its primary obligations protecting the orthodoxy of this teaching. Earlier ages apparently found his insurrection against his father too problematic to celebrate. Veneration of Hermenegild was extended to the entire Church in the papacy of Urban VIII in the early 1600s.[9] It seems likely that the Spanish Hapsburgs at that time were anxious to strengthen the connections between their German roots and the Germanic roots (Visigoths) of the early Spanish monarchy. Sor Juana is undoubtedly appreciative of this motive as she has her characters bow to the Spanish King Charles II, his French wife María Luisa de Bourbon, and Austrian Queen Mother Maríana at the opening of a play designed to honor the Spanish monarchy as defenders of orthodoxy, by pointing to an early Spanish prince of Germanic origin who died for the faith. It was also a way for Sor Juana to pay tribute to her patroness, the countess of Paredes, who included Hermenegild among her ancestors.[10]

The obvious explicit reference to "the sacrament" comes near the end of the play when Hermenegild, in his prison cell, resists the temptation to receive communion from the Arian bishop even though his refusal will cost him his life. Editor Méndez Plancarte laments what he sees as theological lapses in Sor Juana's construction of the scene between the Arian bishop, Apostasia, and Hermenegild, the Christian prince, because Hermenegild appears to be implying that the communion he would be receiving from the bishop would not be licit due to the bishop's invalid consecration.[11] While it is true that the validity of episcopal orders was not an issue between Christians and Arians in the sixth century, it was an issue between Catholics and Protestants in the seventeenth: as George Tavard has noted, to Sor Juana's audience "the Arians were the Protestants." The royal audience to whom the play was dedicated, as well as the censors, would have immediately understood this reference.[12]

Indeed in the final discussion between the Bishop Apostasia and Hermenegild, Sor Juana indicates her familiarity with both the tridentine texts on the Eucharist as well as on ordination. Apostasia points out that the validity of the sacrament is independent of the moral worthiness of the priest, which the Council of Trent had affirmed. But Hermenegild objects to receiving the Eucharist from the Arian bishop on juridical grounds: he is not in union with the bishop of Rome and, therefore, lacks apostolic succession. Hermenegild's receiving communion from the hand of the Arian bishop would not be the sign of unity it should be.

In addition to the overarching theme of martyrdom for the sake of the truth of the sacrament, there are numerous other explicit references to eucharistic doctrine. In the opening scene, Faith calls forth the virtues of Mercy, Peace, and Justice, which "appear to be contradictory," so that Truth can purify them. Faith then introduces herself as the foundation of the Church, and a virtue especially necessary for the belief in the presence of the Body and Blood of the Lord in the Eucharist. She is a blind virtue, who works where sight is not sufficient, and she must be especially operative at the "sovereign Table" where Christ gives us his Blood and Flesh as food" (OC 3:119). Sor Juana makes the nice point that all the other mysteries, such as the Incarnation of the Divine Word, the Virgin Birth, are at least in part "visible." The humanity of Jesus is manifest, as is the pregnancy of the Virgin, but the Bread and Wine have no visible resemblance to what they signify. In fact by insisting on the paradox of the real presence of Christ in the bread and wine which were only apparently bread and wine, but really Body and Blood of Christ in the teaching on the Eucharist, the limits of what are considered physical and spiritual were stretched and blurred. What was conceived of as most "real" is the most physical "corporeal" aspects of Christ's person, his body and blood, yet this most physical presence is manifest only in an appearance, i.e. the Bread and Wine, which were no longer really what they appeared to be physically, that is bread and wine.

Virtues can remain in harmony on an abstract level, but come into conflict in concrete application. One of the fruits of the Eucharist is an increase in virtue. Hermenegild can be seen to be representative of one who, nourished by the sacrament, grows in virtue. The allegorical character Faith invites others (Peace, Justice, Mercy, and Truth) to test Hermenegild's constancy. They do battle in his conscience on the basis of conflicting scriptural passages.[13] The commandments include honoring father and mother, but Jesus said he had come to bring conflict between father and son. Jesus proclaimed he came to bring peace to the Kingdom, but Justice demands the cutting off of the offending member (here understood as Hermenegild's duty to cut himself off from his father's heretical kingdom) (OC 3:122–23). The prince searches in his heart for the "bond of all the virtues," charity or love, while he is beset by conflicting loves, that for his father and his ancestors, and that of his obligations to his Christian wife and son (the future), and his new community, the Catholic Church. He cries out to the personified virtues, echoing Augustine.[14] "If there is a bond which links you, it is Charity: How is it that in me you appear opposites?"

The anguished dream of Hermenegild's conscience contrasts with his father's waking dream of the greatness of his dynasty, and its faithfulness to the Arian tradition. Fantasy, representing the king's own melancholy imagination, sets the stage for a play within a play set in the royal throne room. "Spain," with royal cloak and imperial scepter, is armed and seated on the throne. Beside him sits Fame, singing, who orchestrates the appearance of the Leovigild's predecessors. There, not love, but the spilling of blood has been the bond of the dynasty (OC 3:146–51).

Sor Juana can be seen to be building on Thomas Aquinas when she portrays Hermenegild as embodying three things signified by the Eucharist. The first is the Passion of Christ, which Hermenegild represents in his suffering death as a martyr. The second is the "divine and heavenly grace" imparted to the soul to nurture it in virtue and love. This Hermenegild demonstrates both through his struggle with the virtues and through his sacrifice of family happiness for the virtue of Faith. Aquinas's third level of meaning of the Eucharist is as "a foreshadowing of future eternal joy and glory." This Sor Juana indicates in the final scene where the Virtues celebrate Hermenegild before an altar displaying the Host and the Chalice. Earth shall weep at its loss, but heaven rejoices. Hermenegild in his person has united the virtues. He is now invoked to help his descendants, i.e., the currently reigning Catholic monarchs of Spain to follow his example (OC 3: 181–83).

COMPLEXITIES OF CONVERSION

WHEN THE *auto* and its *loa* are seen as a unit together, other levels of significance emerge which would have encouraged the audience to consider the complexities of conversion and meditate on the ironies of history. In the *loa* two "strong men" enter to interrupt a theological discussion on the greatest benefits of Christ's love. One is the ancient hero Hercules, who sets up two columns representing "the pillars of Hercules," thought to be the limit of the land surface of the earth, but also metaphorically indicating the limits of knowledge of the old world (OC 3:104–5). The other is Columbus returning from his first voyage to the Americas. His *albricias* or "good news" (gospel) to Europe is that there are "more empires/ which your arms can enslave and subject." In images recalling rape, he describes his "rudder breaking the seal which Abila and Calpe, the two cliffs of the straits of Gibraltar, had maintained closed. "The torrid zone is alive to the benefits of Heaven!" (OC 3:106–7). A soldier proclaims that the pillars of Hercules, just set up, should be taken down and the "trophies" of Columbus set in their place.

Through the celebration of "the founding saint of the Spanish monarchy," Saint Hermenegild, Sor Juana has opened up the discussion of the conversion of the Americas in a number of ways. First, she shows the difficulties conversion can involve. Hermenegild must abandon his past. Second, she reminds the audience that "Catholic Spain" was not always "Catholic," and that sixteen generations of kings claimed allegiance to the perfidious Arian heresy. Third, arguments for the unity of Europe based on religious unity, are found in the mouths of Arian characters. This was also the dream of Charles V of Spain, also Charles V, Holy Roman Emperor, during the religious upheaval of the previous century. The Arian bishop, Apostasia, argues that resistance to conversion should be met with armed force, an argument made periodically by the Spanish crown, not only in the early days of colonization, but even in Sor Juana's own lifetime.

MONUMENTS OF FAITH

A READER OF the 1692 volume would move from the end of *The Martyr*, where the choir composed of Faith, Peace, Mercy, Truth, and Justice bows to the Spanish court, to the *loa* for *The Scepter of Joseph*, and again to the "New World." The opening words of the second *loa* are those of Music, describing Natural Law as she welcomes "the new sun of faith, which gilds the high mountains" of the New World (OC 3:184). A conversation develops among the ladies, Faith, Law of Grace, Natural Law, and Nature, in which they congratulate each other on their happy cooperation in "the new conversion of the conquered Indies" (OC 3:186). With this turn of phrase, Sor Juana has located this exchange not in the original evangelization effort of the sixteenth century, but in her own time when, as Méndez Plancarte explains, missionary work was still under way in "many parts of our land." In 1680 the missions in what was then referred to as New Basque Country (Arizona and New Mexico) had been destroyed by the Pueblo Indians. It was not until 1690 that a military invasion allowed the reestablishment of the missions, and the subjugation of the Indians.[15] Sor Juana had apparently met the Jesuit Padre Kino, one of the most famous missionaries to the northern regions of New Spain and had written a poem in his honor (OC 1:205).

Faith laments the centuries of the "humiliation of the Indies under blind Idolatry," who caused the natives to violate the precepts of natural law by staining the altars with human blood thereby revealing themselves the most barbarous of human beings, more cruel than animals, because they turn against their own kind. The ladies agree that they should erect a monument in honor of their own missionary success. The word here is *padrón*, which more specifically signifies a "column or pillar with an commemorative inscription,"[16] thus recalling the pillars of Hercules erected in the *loa* preceding *The Martyr of the Sacrament: St. Hermenegild*. The ladies differ about the type of monument which would be most appropriate. Nature would be most pleased by the demolition of the altars where so much blood was shed. Natural Law, because of her revulsion at the Indian practice of polygamy, prefers to see the new law making the first wife the legitimate one, as the sign of missionary success. Grace is interested in stripping the altars of the false gods and replacing them with the image of Christ. Faith agrees with Grace, adding that the ultimate sign of the mystery of Christian faith, the Eucharist, symbolized by a Chalice and a Host, should be placed on the purified altars (the last image in the preceding play). They all congratulate each other on this solution and, in an extended chorus, invoke the heavenly choirs of angels to complete their celebration.

The heavenly hosts, however, do not descend; instead, the enraged Idolatry dressed as an Indian woman enters fuming: "No, as long as my rage lives, Faith, you will not achieve your purpose" (OC 3:192). With a stroke, the theological discussion is challenged out of its self-enclosed smug satisfaction. Idolatry charges her Christian accusers of introducing conflict into a peaceful empire, enslaving peoples and forcing them to embrace all new doctrines without understanding. Even if Faith and her companions manage to obliterate the altars, Idolatry maintains, they will not be able to destroy the idea behind them. Even if they insist that there is one unique God to be adored, and supposing that the Indians, in fact, do adore this one divinity, they still have not contradicted the precept that was the basis of human sacrifice. She continues, using an explanation of Las Casas:[17] God demands the best, most noble sacrifice, the human being. According to Las Casas the error of the Indians was not in the idea of sacrifice, but in the object they chose (OC 3:193–94). The ensuing points made by Nature, Law of Grace, and Natural Law are spoken from a context that Idolatry is aware she cannot penetrate. "I don't understand such matters. Being a barbarian (*barbara*) I lack the principles from which to answer you" (OC 3:194). Her objections to the abolition of human sacrifice still stand: God needs to be offered the most noble sacrifice in order to be satisfied: and the eating of the sacrifice contributes to long life. Faith finally agrees but argues that the purest offering is not only human but also divine. Only such a sacrifice would really satisfy God and give eternal life. Such a sacrifice is commemorated in the Eucharist.

Idolatry maintains that, although she has been *partly catechized* (OC 3:198), this mystery still escapes her. Faith suggests that they put on an allegorical play that will show how prophecy made visible this sacred mystery. Finally, the Christian characters all agree that the best monument is the one erected in the souls of the faithful, as they venerate the Eucharist. And with that, the stage is set for the "historical allegory," *El Cetro de José* (The Scepter of Joseph).[18]

THE SCEPTER OF JOSEPH

THE BIBLICAL STORY of Joseph, son of Jacob/Israel, the father of the twelve tribes, which is the basis of this *auto* (Gn 37:39–45), contains many elements seen by early theologians as prefiguring Christ. Sor Juana integrates these into her play. In the opening lines, Joseph's brothers' voices offstage announce: "There the dreamer has been thrown into the pit, and we will see if we put him to death, of what use his dreams are" (OC 3:201–2). Here, the connection between Jesus and Joseph is immediately established. The passage combines the plight of the suffering prophet Jeremiah who was thrown into a pit and left for dead (Jer 38:5–10) and the words of the 22d Psalm "He threw himself on the Lord: let the Lord deliver him for He holds him dear" (Ps 22:9), which Jesus' enemies, the scribes and pharisees, used to mock him on the cross (Mk 15:31–32; Lk 24:35).

Unlike Adam (Gn 3) and like Jesus (Mt 4:1–11) Joseph resists temptation, as represented in the incident with Potiphar's wife. Joseph, who had the appearance of a slave, was elevated to the right hand of the king (pharaoh), like Jesus who took the form of a slave to be raised up to his Father (Phil 2:7–9). Joseph is hailed as the "saviour of the world" who gives the people "daily bread" (OC 3:232) in times of famine, a foreshadowing of the bread of the Eucharist which will feed both body and soul (OC 3:233). The table at which Joseph eats with his twelve brothers prefigures the table of the Eucharist, and the brothers the twelve disciples. The bread will become Bread of Life in the Eucharist; the ritual washing of feet before the meal prefigures Christ's washing the feet of his disciples. Finally, the scepter of Joseph, which Jacob kisses as he dies, is decorated with a loaf of bread, while Jacob, in a deathbed intuition, sees the union with his flesh of the One who is to be the blessing for all nations.

Sor Juana includes vignettes of other biblical events, which serve to recall more general aspects of the sacrament: It is intended for the redemption from sin, and it is the sacrament of faith *par excellence* (OC 3:189). In the first case, God (as the character *Musica*) invokes punishment on Adam and the Serpent. Though Adam will "earn his bread by the sweat of his brow," ultimately the Serpent will be crushed by the heel of the Woman. In the second case, Abraham, the model of the faithful believer (Rom 4), is shown under the stars, pondering the paradox of his childlessness in the face of God's promise that through his offspring all nations will be blessed. Like the promise sustaining Abraham, the Eucharist was also seen as the Bread (viaticum) nourishing the believers on their journey to the heavenly Kingdom.[19] A third scene recapitulates this motif. In it Jacob wakes from his dream of the celestial ladder and demands bread for the remainder of his journey.

Sor Juana surrounds the story of Joseph with an allegorical framework. Fallen angelic intelligence—symbolized by the characters Lucifer, his beautiful wife Intelligencia, his friends and constant companions Sciencia and Envidia (Envy), and his daughter Conjectura—attempt in vain to discern the salvific meaning of events. Prophecy, their adversary, sounds forth the future significance of the unfolding drama. A battle of wits of cosmic dimensions unfolds that has implications for other questions: the role of evil in the world; the possibility of redemption; the limits of intelligence without faith to interpret scripture; the ability of faith to see the workings of divine grace in the events of history and, therefore, by implication the presence of Christ, in the Eucharist. Prophecy in the finale encourages the audience to rejoice in the light of the knowledge they possess which the ancients possessed only in hope, and the Jews only partially: the knowledge of the bread which nourishes for eternity.

CONQUEST AND CONVERSION

THE *LOA* FOR *The Divine Narcissus* moves back to the era of the conquest again revealing Sor Juana's awareness of the complexities of the history of the conversion of the Mexican peoples. With remarkable compactness she captures the phases of the relationship between the missionaries and the conquistadors in the sixteenth century. The characters are two couples: Occidente (the West) and America, dressed in festive Indian dress; and Religion, a Spanish lady, and Celo (Furious Zeal), an armed conquistador. The Spanish couple stumbles onto the Indians celebrating the great god of the seeds in song and dance.[20] After looking on for a while, Religion chides Zeal for not being offended by the idolatry he sees. The conquistador assures his consort that soon he will avenge the insults to her.[21] As the Indians enter again singing and dancing, Religion holds him back saying she needs to try to convince them peaceably before he unleashes his fury. She then proceeds to tell America and Occidente that the Indians' religion is the work of the devil, and demands they open their eyes and believe the true doctrine. America and Occidente conclude she is crazy and continue their dancing.[22] Zeal, furious at the insult to his "gentle beloved spouse," threatens violence. When America and Occidente refuse to believe him, he and his soldiers attack. In a stylized dance of battle the Spanish couple advances, the American couple retreats and, finally, surrenders. Zeal is ready to kill them at once, but Religion cries out, "I need them alive" (OC 3:11). She explains to the astonished Zeal that his role was to vanquish, hers to use gentle persuasion. Both America and Occidente on hearing this, protest that they will not be so easily persuaded. Though vanquished they still have their free will to keep to their own beliefs. They would rather suffer martyrdom than give up their veneration of their great god of the seeds.

Only at this point does Religion ask them about their beliefs in order to learn how to better persuade them of the truths of the Catholic faith.[23] In the conversation which follows, the Indian couple explain their devotion to their gods, describing the ceremonies and customs which baffled and intrigued the Christian missionaries among the Aztecs: reverence for the priesthood, a type of baptism, individual confession of sins, and absolution. They even explain human sacrifice and its attendant ceremonies, including a meal after the sacrifice in which cakes in the form of human figures made of seeds held together by a paste of victims' blood were consumed. America argues the *reasonableness* of human sacrifice based on the idea that the best life was to be given back to God in order to sustain life, an argument also found in Las Casas' 1550 *Defense of the Indians* and in the *loa* to *The Scepter of Joseph*.[24] Religion counters by demonstrating that the Aztec beliefs in baptism, confession, and a sacrificial meal have superior equivalents in Christianity, and proposes that Occidente and America watch a play. There they will see the prefiguring of the mysteries of the Holy Eucharist in the history of other pagans (the Romans) and will come to understand that this same God is behind their own religious customs.

Though the fiction of the preface play is that the sacramental drama, *El Divino Narciso*, will teach the Indians the mysteries of the Catholic doctrine of the eucharist, it is again clear that the play is really intended to convince the audience at the Spanish court of the dignity and piety of the Indians and of the complexity of their history, customs, and religion.

One senses Sor Juana's political awareness in the dialogue at the end of the *loa*. Religion makes a point of saying the play will be performed in Madrid, "center of the Faith and the royal seat of the Catholic kings to whom the Indies owe the light of the Gospel" (OC 3:19). Zeal, the conquistador, still objects that it does not seem proper to write something in Mexico which will be performed in another place. To which Religion answers with another question: "Has it never been the case that something is made in one place to be useful in another?" (OC 3:19). Though she does not say it directly, it is clear that this was the relationship of Christianity to Mexican culture. She then adds that this is not her idea, but something she is doing under obedience. Zeal asks again more pointedly, "Why introduce the Indies in order to take them to Madrid?" (OC 3:19–20). Religion then replies that the persons introduced were not real, but abstractions which could easily be transported from one place to another. Here again, in a subtle manner, Sor Juana is asking the audience to abstract from the concrete to the general, suggesting that ideas transcend physical boundaries, and, by implication, what comes from Mexico can be understood in Madrid (OC 3:20). Finally all the characters with flattering words make deep bows to the king and queen and their courtiers. The *loa* ends as the characters return to the fiction that the following play is intended to teach the Indians. *All the characters*, Indians and Spaniards, exit dancing and singing: "Blessed be the day that I learned of the great God of the Seeds!" (OC 3:21).[25]

THE DIVINE NARCISSUS

SOR JUANA'S THIRD eucharistic drama, *The Divine Narcissus*, begins with two women entering dressed as peasant girls: Synagogue and Paganism, each with her accompanying chorus of peasant girls and shepherds. Again, by use of this "accepted" mix of two religions,

Sor Juana makes a sotto voce plea for a similar respect for Aztec mythology. Synagogue sings the praises of "the Lord of all humans" (a variation of the first line of Psalm 116, "Praise the Lord all you peoples"). Paganism applauds Narcissus and his divine beauty. Human Nature, also a woman, enters dressed "in a beautiful manner" as befits "the mother of both of them, according to natural law" (OC 3:26). She addresses both and proposes to present an allegory which will take its meaning from Synagogue and its voice from Paganism. In a second rendering of the relationship, she says that Synagogue will "give a body to the idea" that Paganism will dress (OC 3:27). Though maintaining on the surface the conventional ordering of revealed over natural religion, a shift from a clear primacy of revealed religion is introduced through the costuming of the allegorical figures and through their description in terms of family relationships. Furthermore, as their mother, Natura Humana speaks to them both equally as her daughters. Though she first describes Paganism as a "perishable beauty" (OC 3:25) and Synagogue as "certain in the discourses of her prophets" (OC 3:25), she goes on to remind them (and the audience) that a time will come when they will change places, an obvious reference to the rejection of the gospel by the Jews and its acceptance by the pagans. Concluding her assignment of roles, Human Nature introduces one of the major ideas the play wishes to convey: "Through their frequent conformity divine and human letters tell us that the highest mysteries can begin to come into view even through the pen of pagans" (OC 3:26).

This idea is reinforced as the play combines the story of Narcissus in Ovid's *Metamorphosis* and that of Jesus in the Gospels. Sor Juana stays close to the plot of the fable, even incorporating in poetic paraphrase parts of Ovid's text. Yet her use of biblical material gives a distinctive cast to the personality of Narcissus. Narcissus is not a hunter, but the good shepherd of the Gospels: as in the Lukan parable, he goes off in search of the one lost sheep (Human Nature), and as in John's Gospel, when he dies he becomes the shepherd who gives his life for his sheep.

Examination of the *patterning* of traditional themes, images, and arguments in *El Divino Narciso* reveals that Sor Juana is presenting theological positions, that challenged standard notions of post-Tridentine theology by relativizing the relationship between natural and revealed religion and by stressing the universality of divine salvific will. Like Las Casas, Sor Juana insists on the equality of all humanity, pagans and Christians. The closing words of the *loa* above mirror the second play's opening refrain: "Praise to the Lord of all humanity!" (OC 3:22). The great god of the seeds (also understood as the Lord of the Eucharist) is the God of all humanity. The play insists on this idea through its eleven repetitions of this refrain in the first two scenes.

The correspondence between the two religions, Pagan (Aztec) and Christian, is further underscored if we look at the opening setting of the *loa* and the closing of *El Divino Narciso*. The *loa* begins with a hymn on the Aztec equivalent of the Corpus Christi feast,[26] and the sacramental drama ends with Human Nature leading all the characters in a paraphrase of the "Pange, lingua," the great hymn composed by Thomas Aquinas on the mystery of the Eucharist, especially associated with the Corpus Christi feast. Sor Juana also alters the standard prayer, praising the Trinity in the final verses of the play, replacing the Spirit with "Love which proceeds from both" Father and Son, thus ending the play with the word which best describes the Divine Narcissus, who for love of humanity ran the risk of death. For according to Sor Juana, "Even God in the world finds no loves without danger" (OC 3:93).

4

Mary as Divine (M)other

There is not one day when I awake, that among the other
benefits for which I give thanks, that I do not thank Him
especially for creating His Mother, and myself in the law of
grace where I enjoy her protection . . .

(OC 4:781–95/495)

DIVINE PROTECTRESS OF THE AMERICAS

The veneration of the "Virgin of Guadalupe" on the site of the Aztec earth goddess Tonantzin on the hill of Tepeyac near Mexico City, began in the middle of the sixteenth century and had been part of Mexican piety for over a century when Sor Juana was born in 1648. Scholars today see this image of the Virgin as a composite of Christian and Aztec symbols which served to make Christianity less foreign and more acceptable to indigenous peoples. The *Nican Mopohua*, a Nahuatl (Aztec) version of the apparitions, was published in 1649 by Luis Lasso de la Vega, chaplain of the Guadalupe shrine from 1646 to 1656.[1] According to this account, a beautiful lady describing herself as coming from "the one true God, the God who gives life"[2] speaks to the middle-aged Indian, Juan Diego, and commissions him to go to the bishop to convey her wish that a temple be built on the site of her apparition. After two futile attempts to convince the bishop, Juan Diego is ready to give up, but in a third appearance the lady says she will give him a convincing sign. She tells him to gather roses from the hillside where the church is to be built. Juan Diego takes the marvelous roses, suddenly growing on the previously barren hillside, to the bishop in his *tilma* or Indian cape. When he opens it, a mysterious image of the Virgin is imprinted there. This sign convinced the bishop, and the shrine was constructed.

Given her sensitivity to indigenous customs and languages, and given what has been termed her incipient Mexican nationalism, Sor Juana's near total neglect of the Virgin of Guadalupe, symbol of Mexican nationalism, and emblem of the conversion of the indigenous, is difficult to fathom. This is all the more so because the nun's awareness of the dynamic of effective evangelizing is especially clear in her only poem which mentions the Guadalupe Virgin. It praises an epic poem to the Virgin by Father Fransicso de Castro, S.J. The sonnet reveals not only that Sor Juana was familiar with the image and its foundational narrative, but that she is clearly aware of its function in translating Aztec (Mexican) cultural symbols into more acceptable Spanish (Castillian) ones:

> The Marvel made of flowers
> divine American Protectress,
> which, in order to be,
> passed over the Mexican rose
> to appear as Rose of Castille.
>
> (OC 1:310)

Sor Juana demonstrates her awareness of the translation process through her development of the image of flowers, celestial bodies, and the role of intelligence. In the shrine's foundational narrative, the first sign of the authenticity of Juan Diego's visions were the roses (the flower traditionally associated with Mary) growing on the stony ground of Tepeyac. Flowers also played an extremely important role in the Aztec religious world as a symbol for truth.[3] Flower and song were the means of communicating truths to the heart, which was the seat of intelligence.[4]

Thus when Sor Juana writes of the "marvel made of flowers, divine Protectress of the Americas," flowers point obviously to the proof of the roses, both on the mountain, and those taken to the bishop in the cape of Juan Diego, but they can also be seen to refer to the the translation of images of which the image of the Virgin of Guadalupe was a model.

The second stanza compares apocalyptic symbols from the Old World (Patmos) with those of the New World shrine at Tepeyac.

Rather than the dragon
whose rebel neck and haughty tread
there at Patmos, (the Old World) was humbled,
here (Mexico) sovereign intelligence reigns,
of her pure greatness the pure seat.

The Guadalupe image features an angel supporting the base on which Mary stands. In European scholastic theology, angels were understood to be "pure intelligence." In the Aztec system, the heavenly creature supporting the base heightened the divine significance of the image "because royalty and representatives of the deities were carried by others."[5] The final stanza picks up the threads of the associations the Aztecs would make with the truth conveying power of flowers and song (poetry).

. . . and Heaven, which the mysterious copy
a second time with its celestial signs
adds up in figures of flowers
a second time;
no less a beautiful translation,
is rendered by your verses unequalled,
by the marvel of your cultured pen.

The expression "celestial signs" suggests the rays of the sun surrounding the image, and the moon under the feet of the image, as well as the stars which decorate the mantle of the Virgin, their shape evocative of flowers.

There are several passages in her work that, however, can be read as implicit references to Guadalupe. One possible key is found in the Nahuatl hymn in the 1676 *villancicos* for the Assumption (OC 2:17), where the Indians call the Virgin "Tonantzin," the Nahuatl title given to the virgin mother earth Goddess, Cihuacóatl, whose shrine had been at the site of the apparition to Juan Diego. Even today, as Alan R. Sandstrom, reporting on his recent anthropological findings, writes: " When the Nahua speak in Spanish they refer to Tonantsi as the Virgin of Guadalupe, for in their minds Tonantsi and the Virgin are the same."[6] Thus, Sor Juana may have been intending an oblique reference to Guadalupe in this Indian title. Another possible reference to the Virgin of Guadalupe may be based on an understanding of "guadalupe" as a transformation of the Nahuatl title "tlecuauhtlacupeuh," meaning "she who comes flying from the region of light like an eagle of fire." The region of light was the dwelling place of the Aztec gods, and the eagle was a sign from the gods.[7] We find one such example in the *Ejercicios de la Encarnación,* where Sor Juana dwells at length on the image of Mary as "Queen of birds." Mary is asked to

> teach us so that our affection flies to you and, like the eagle who teaches her eaglets to fly and who flies above them, encourage the flight of our contemplation so that we drink the rays of the sun of justice, and defend us from the infernal serpent beneath your wings . . . so that, after our death, we will fly in your company to the heights of glory where we will clearly enjoy the light which the Lord gives in the beatific vision.
> (OC 4:488)[8]

A third key *may be* be in the frequent references to Mary as the *morena* or dark one, a description associated with the beloved in the Song of Songs ("I am dark but comely"), but also in the Mexican context with the Indian aspect of the Guadalupe Virgin. For example, the fifth poem for the Feast of the Assumption (1676), which builds on the Song of Songs, portrays the Virgin as a young shepherdess "whose dark color illuminates the sun's rays" (OC 2:9). This image is, certainly, also reminiscent of the Guadalupe figure surrounded with the sun's rays. Most frequently, in Sor Juana's work, Mary is designated as the *morena* by characters speaking a *negro* dialect. In the eighth poem, one character says to another: "She is not white like you . . . doesn't she say: I am darkened from the rays of the Sun?" (OC 2:105–6).

Other implicit references may be found under the mantle of the mysterious woman in the book of Revelation. Rafael Catalá has shown that other Mexican poets, contemporaneous with Sor Juana (Sigüenza y Góngora, Ramírez de Vargas, Salazar y Torres, and Francisco de Castro), when using apocalyptic imagery associated with the woman in Revelation, do so *explicitly* in the context of the apparitions at Tepeyac.[9] George Tavard suggests that Sor Juana's references to "the woman of the apocalypse" (Rv 12) are, in fact, implicit references to the Virgin of Guadalupe.[10] The woman of the apocalypse, who slew the dragon, was brilliant like the sun, and had the moon under her feet, has obvious similarities with the image of Our Lady of Guadalupe, who is surrounded with rays like the sun, and is standing on the moon. In the Aztec context, the sun's rays would be "read" by natives as references to their sun god, the moon attributed to their goddess of fertility. The apocalyptic woman is in the pains of labor. Mary, in the Guadalupe image, is the pregnant mother.

However, these few indications still do not explain why Sor Juana fails to take advantage of the figure of the Virgin of Guadalupe. This omission is even more intriguing when we consider that her longest sequence of religious poems (thirty two of them) was composed for the dedication of the church for the convent of Conceptionist nuns. It was dedicated both to Saint Bernard of Clairvaux, and at the request of their benefactors to "Our Lady of Guadalupe." Even though Sor Juana alludes to these benefactors, D. José and D. Domingo de Retes, in several of the poems (OC 2:442), she makes no mention of the apparitions at Tepeyac. George Tavard sees Sor Juana's avoidance of direct reference as "part of her baroque conceptism," which avoids mention of individual Marian shrines and prefers to remain at the level of " theological content related to the mysteries of Christ . . ."[11] It is also possible that there was resistance from within her order to the explicit naming of the Mexican Virgin of Guadalupe in Mexico, since the Hieronimites were the keepers of the shrine of the Spanish Virgin of Guadalupe in Estremadura.

MARY AS MOTHER OF GOD

THIS RESERVE IS also curious because in general it can be said that Sor Juana's sensitivity to traditions, literary, social, and religious is perhaps nowhere more evident than in her exquisite elaboration and joyous rendering of devotion to Mary. Nearly all of the nun's religious poems are connected to Mary in some form. Except for her two sequences for the Feast of St. Peter (1677 and 1683), all are either for Marian feasts such as the Assumption (1671, 1679, 1685, 1690), the Immaculate Conception (1676, 1689), the Presentation of Mary in the Temple (3 poems: OC 2:217–21), the Annunciation (OC 2:221–24), or related to events (Christmas, 1689) or people connected with Mary (St. Joseph, 1690) or with male saints who had a special devotion to Mary (Peter Nolascus, 1677; Bernard of Clairvaux, 1690).

At the time of Sor Juana's construction of the triumphal arch, she had already contributed to the public religious life of the city through a series of compositions known as *villancicos*, most of them for Marian feasts. Originating in the medieval Spanish folk tradition, *villancicos* had become a form of sacred music sung in Spanish to replace the Latin responsories in the recitation of matins. They were ideally suited to teaching a broad nonliterate audience and reflect the nun's connection with elements of the "popular religion" of her day. They incorporated a wide variety of verse forms, minor dramatic dialogues, and satirical humorous elements.[12] It is here that we find Sor Juana's poems or parts of poems in *negro* dialect, Nahuatl, Portuguese, and even Basque, reflecting the mix of populations which would be in attendance at church services.

As a result, the form itself of Sor Juana's religious poetry is celebratory through its music, its drama, its public nature, and its popular and humorous elements.[13] Furthermore, it is celebratory *ritual* taking place within a set arena, in this case the cathedral, defined by community practices (that of solemn vespers the evening before a great feast) and determined by a literary as well as religious tradition.[14] Because the bulk of her religious poetry consists in this form, it again breaks out of the private forum of the mystical, or individually devotional, into the public forum as liturgical and communal. Her celebration of Mary reflects the New Testament description of the good scribe "instructed in the Kingdom of Heaven" who selects old and new from his storeroom (Mt 14:52). Sor Juana builds on old traditions, transforming them to correspond in significant ways to the interest of today's religious aspirations.

Contrary to what one might expect, Sor Juana's emphasis on Mary is not typical of major women religious writers. Though Marian piety is one of the identifying marks of Catholicism, evidence of her role in the works of outstanding women religious writers has been ambivalent. She is considered in a minor way, if at all, in the writings of Catherine of Sienna, Julian of Norwich, and Teresa of Ávila.[15] A study by Donald Bell and Rudolf Weinstein covering the period from 1000 to 1700 reveals that only about a third of the female saints were characterized as especially devoted to Mary.[16] Based on this data, Carolyn Walker Bynum concludes that it cannot be maintained "that women turned especially to female figures as mediators."[17]

Later in 1690, when defending her right to theological reflection in her autobiographical *Response*, Sor Juana maintains that her only two published "theological works" were the *Ejercicios de la Encarnación* (Exercises on the Incarnation) and *Ofrecimientos de los dolores* (Offerings on the Sorrows of Mary) printed "years ago" for the edification of her sisters, adding that she was inspired to write them because "things connected to most holy Mary are bound to enflame the most frozen heart" (OC 4:474.1400–1401).

Sor Juana renders enthusiastic tribute to Mary as Mother of God. Official church doctrine has always maintained that Christ is the only mediator of salvation, as was reaffirmed in the Second Vatican Council's warning against the tendency of the faithful to exaggerate Mary's importance.[18] Two of Sor Juana's interpreters have criticized what they consider to be an exaggerated Marian emphasis. Marié Cécile Bénassy-Berling, commenting that "if the virgin is not deified she is the object of overwhelming enthusiasm," notes that some of the liberties that poetic license of the *villancico* allows might shock unsuspecting readers.[19] George Tavard is more concerned with what might appear to be overstepping the bounds of orthodoxy: "Her emphasis on Mary's privileges . . . conveys the impression of taking away the uniqueness and exclusiveness of Christ as the one 'Mediator of the new Covenant.'"[20] Elizabeth Johnson has offered another possible interpretation of Sor Juana's vivid interest in Mary:

> . . . wherever Mary is described or addressed in such a way that the ultimacy of the divine as reflected in Scripture, doctrine or liturgy is evoked, or wherever the ultimacy of the believer's trust is correspondingly elicited, there it can be supposed that the reality of God is being named in female metaphors.[21]

A comparison of Sor Juana's interpretation with the conventional rendering of Mary in effect shows her feminist consciousness at work, taking advantage of material of traditional Mariology and popular devotion to create a religious symbolic system that has at its center a female figure of power and radiance, nearly a goddess. In so doing Sor Juana can be said to "be mining the golden mother lode of the Marian tradition in order to retrieve female imagery and language about the holy mystery of God."[22]

Some of Sor Juana's rhetorical strategies, as well as her selection of those qualities of Mary's personality and aspects of the tradition of her cult which correspond to contemporary feminists' analysis of feminine gendered speech, create openings in traditional language about God to a degree too remarkable to be purely accidental. We even find manipulation of grammatical gender when naming the divine. In the second of three poems on the Incarnation of the Word, Sor Juana uses the word *palabra* (feminine gender), rather than the more customary masculine *verbo*," for Word. As a result, the divine word made flesh becomes *ella* (her) in its pronominal form. Although in Romance languages there is no necessary association of grammatical gender with male/female sex, the repeated use of a word of feminine gender in a context in which normally a masculine one would be used, as is the case in this poem, stands out. Furthermore, the use of the pronoun *ella*, especially when distanced from its referent noun, has the effect of connecting the discourse with feminine reality. Editor Méndez Plancarte, reveals his discomfort at this unusual usage and takes pains to "correct" it six times in his notes on the first thirty lines of this poem.[23] He also refers the reader to another of her poems in which the "same mistake" is made.[24]

In order to appreciate more exactly the specific character of this aspect of Sor Juana's Marian piety, we need to remember that Marian devotions were seen as an integral part of the true faith of Catholics, as opposed to heretical Lutherans and Calvinists who considered them idolatrous. Just as Sor Juana, in her liturgical poetry, is following the literary traditions of the immensely popular and highly developed *villancico*, so too, in her Mariology, she is part of a theological tradition which exalts Mary and emphasizes her power.

MARY AND CREATION

THOUGH SHE CLAIMS in the *Response* to have written *The Exercises on the Incarnation* for her sisters in the convent, in the text itself she proceeds with a minimum of fuss to claim authority to be writing for priests as well as for her sisters, in strong contrast to the elaborate apology with which she would later preface her explicitly theological *Athenagoric Letter*.[25] Indeed, in the closing exercise she directs "the priests that pray in their homes to pray kneeling the Divine Office, at least Vespers, in honor of such a great mystery" (OC 4:506). She also makes a point of saying that the exercises are structured so that "all types of people" may be able to do them "for their benefit and for the honor of the Lord" (OC 4:477). The recommended readings and prayers, as well as pious practices that accompany each day's meditations, are different for those "who know how to read Latin" and those who do not. As the novena progresses, the nun devotes ever increasing space to "those who do not read Latin."

It is significant that Sor Juana begins her novena with a reference to the famous mystic and advisor of Spain's King Phillip IV

(1621–65), Mother María de Jesús (María Coronal de Ágreda, 1602–65). The Franciscan nun's treatise, *Mystical City of God*, uses "city of God" as the primary metaphor for Mary, as Ágreda narrates her visions of Mary's life. Though Sor Juana takes the idea that God showed Mary the creation of the universe from Ágreda's second volume, *The Incarnation*,[26] the Mexican nun's expositions, for all their warmth and effusiveness, have as their foundation, primarily metaphors from the Bible and Marian popular devotion, rather than private mystical revelations as does Ágreda's work. Unlike the latter, Sor Juana has each day's exercise contain a scriptural meditation, a prayer or invocation, and an exhortation to the faithful. This is in no way a private or special revelation, but Sor Juana's sensitive intelligence responding to Scripture, the power of the Marian symbol, and the person of Mary.

Indeed, her *exercicios* are structurally more reminiscent of the *Spiritual Exercises* of Ignatius of Loyola than of the great Spanish mystical tradition of Teresa of Ávila and John of the Cross. Like Ignatius, who incidentally also intended his *Exercises* to be elastic enough to include laity, as well as vowed religious,[27] Sor Juana begins each exercise with a meditation, and then moves from prayer to action. She also finishes each day with recommendations on the cultivation of one of the seven cardinal virtues. Ignatius begins his exercises with a meditation from the book of Genesis, which emphasizes the creation of the first humans, their fall from divine favor, and their ejection from Paradise (Gn 1:26–3:3). He encourages the cultivation of the believer's sense of unworthiness before God. Sor Juana uses the seven days creation narrative (Gn 1:1–2:4) as the scriptural starting point for her novena, as well as to structure her praise of Mary into seven sections. Mary's title as Mother of God is interpreted, obviously, far beyond that of "Mother of Jesus." As Mother of God, she is present at the beginning of all things. Mary is not only the perfect woman, but the perfect human being, and God orchestrates creation, to adore her. Celebration of this "stellar" example of humanity, not remorse at sins, is the appropriate response of the faithful.

The Mexican nun's skill as a poet is also evident as each day of the novena focuses on a major image from one of the seven days of creation, playing along a vast register of traditional Marian titles and images to reinforce Mary's sovereignty over creation, as well as her role as mediatrix between God and humanity. Thus on the first day, light, the first creation of God, is described as created to be

Mary's vassal (OC 4:478). She is invoked as Queen of Light, physical and intellectual, making accessible knowledge of the divine essence. Believers are encouraged to direct their eyes to God's most Holy Mother, Queen of Light, herself most radiant, conceived without the darkness of sin. God's mother is also "our Mother," and her intercession is invoked for obtaining the light of grace in the eyes of her divine son. This again contrasts with María of Ágreda, who begins with the "void" and the abyss: light and its relationship to darkness.[28] For Ágreda Mary's infinite dignity as Mother of God had its source in her humility. Her redemptive power derives from this virtue: "this blessed One among women humiliated herself to such an extent, that the most holy Trinity was, as it were, fully paid and satisfied."[29]

God, "infinite Power and immense Wisdom," on the second day places the waters and the vault of heaven as an offering at the "virginal feet" of his mother, because she alone was created like the heavens, between the crystal currents of grace, with no stain of sin. So much more than the heavens does God esteem her that he "exchanged its starry majesty and brilliant canopied throne for the virginal womb, becoming enclosed in this abbreviated and more worthy and beautiful heaven" (OC 4:481). Like water, which is not only pure in itself, but which cleanses others, so Mary is the means of believers' purification. Like the "firmament" she held fast to her course among the erring and wandering apostles, and is celebrated as honor and crown of our humanity (*"nuestro humano ser"*) (OC 4:480).

The dry earth and the sea, creations of the third day, are described as rendering obedience to their queen. The waters which come together are happy to function as symbols of her assembled virtues and qualities. The ocean, in all its grandeur and immensity, with its waves, its caverns, its submarine life, the variety of its denizens, cannot be compared with Mary's exalted virtues. The earth rejoices to be the soil from which such a pure rose will grow (OC 4:481). The roses are happy to be able to symbolize Mary as the center of the universe.[30] In spite of the great favors she was given, Mary remained a model of humility, not as a means of self-deprecation, but because her humility was the cause of her exaltation, and, through imitation of her, the faithful will also be raised to be worthy of praising her titles and privileges eternally.

The great luminaries of the fourth day, the sun and moon, issue forth from the Eternal Idea to greet their Divine Queen who has already been vested with the sun, has the moon under her feet, and is crowned with stars, the "perfect original of the portrait in the Apocalypse" (OC: 4:485). "The stars wanted to crown her but the divine rays of the Holy Trinity were already forming her crown" (OC 4:485). Here, Mary is addressed as Queen of Wisdom, wiser than the queen of Sheba, because she enjoyed the teaching of the true Solomon, possessing true intelligence, which is that of heavenly things. Her womb was the repository of eternal wisdom. Her infused wisdom made her privy to the revolutions of the spheres and all their influences. She knew, through intuition all these things that have exhausted human understanding. The faithful are urged to ask Mary for wisdom. Given the criticisms of Sor Juana because of her learning, it is interesting that the virtue to be cultivated this day is forgiveness of enemies.

The fifth day, which saw the creation of birds and fish, has each praise Mary in its own way. The fish, "with rhetorical silence," praise her as Stella Maris (the Star of the Sea). For the birds, she is Queen of All Winged Creatures. Here, Sor Juana turns to a conventional pun, using the first words of the Latin "Hail Mary," "Ave María," when she calls Mary the "Reina de las Aves" (Queen of the Birds). The royal eagle, who flies to the throne of the Holy Trinity, renders her homage (OC 4:487). As a "heavenly" creature, she has long been compared with birds: the dove that brought the olive branch to Noah, signifying peace between God and humanity; the lofty heron that pursued the Eternal Word and brought it to earth, so that humanity might be satiated with his flesh and blood . . . ; the true phoenix, rising from the ashes of Adam, consumed by the fire of grace; the eagle of God, who teaches her young to fly to the contemplation of the sun of Justice, she defends the faithful from the infernal serpent (OC 4:488).

The sixth day is especially associated with the creation of humanity. Made in God's image, man and woman are still in the state of original justice, which Mary alone of all humankind, subsequently, will enjoy. In this meditation Mary is addressed as the mother and advocate of sinners, the "Queen of humanity, the Honor of nature and the crown of the human race (*del linaje humano*)" (OC 4:491). Through her, the honor lost by Adam is restored. She is "the Glory of Jerusalem, the Joy of Israel and the

Honor of our Christian people, the one who restored the image of God in human nature, the ultimate perfection of all created things." Again, it is Mary who brings God's benefits to humanity through her relationship to her son. Sor Juana exhorts her readers: "Let us swear obedience to our grand Queen . . . our sovereign Empress . . . Let us hurry, not to be outdone by the praise of irrational creatures." She exhorts all to be ready to sacrifice their lives for the Immaculate Conception and for the Holy Gospels of her son.[31] She prays that all will merit seeing Mary "in her Kingdom where she lives and reigns in eternity, with the Most Holy Trinity" (OC 4:492). All peoples are described as "children of God and Mary, and brothers [sic] of Christ our Lord" (OC 4:493).

MARY AND THE HEAVENLY HOSTS

THE DIVINE SABBATH rest on the seventh day is the opening for the development of Mary's relationship to the hierarchy of the heavenly hosts, the angels. Genesis says God rested, but not in the activity of giving favor to Mary. Her privileges break the barriers of nature, extending it to even the pure angelic substances. Mary's title as Queen of Angels is developed in terms of an understanding of angels that sees them as personifying divine attributes. Though the angelic choirs have no definite order or hierarchy (OC 4:494), Sor Juana decides, for the purpose of the last three days of the novena, to divide them into the communications of the attributes of Power, Wisdom, and Love, from the three persons of the Trinity. The seventh day nominally focuses on the prerogative of Power, which is again divided into three choirs: Angels honor God as Spirit; Archangels reveal God as Light; and Virtues work as virtues. Mary is higher than the angels in her participation in the divine essence, she reveals the secrets of God, as well as operating wonders and miracles.

The overlapping order of the angelic choirs soon becomes apparent as, on the eighth day, and at the second level nominally devoted to Wisdom, we again have "Power," this time personified in a category of heavenly messenger, along with "Principalities" and "Dominations." All render obedience to their powerful Queen and Lady. The Powers recognize in Mary the greatest Power, to subject demons, as she alone brought the head of the apocalyptic dragon under her feet. The Principalities appreciate her power to govern and direct kingdoms as does the Church, which sees the words of the Book of Wisdom applying to her: "Through me reign kings, through me princes and the powerful distribute their justice" (OC 4:498). The ninth day considers the third set of angelic choirs: Thrones representing the Justice of God; Cherubim, God's virtues; and Seraphim, God's goodness. Through Mary, the sinless one, all human nature is elevated.

Of its nature, poetry demands a different response from prose, engaging the imagination and the senses more immediately. Sor Juana's poetic genius saves her Mariology from a number of pitfalls in most prose relections on Mary, including even that of the most renowned of Marian devotees, Bernard of Clairvaux. In a number of ways, the *villancico* form, with its range of acceptable poetical styles—lyrical, popular, and dramatic—allows Sor Juana to treat traditional thinking about Mary more obliquely than prose writers and thus to avoid the sometimes grotesque implications of some extremist Marian doctrine. Furthermore, most of Sor Juana's Marian doctrine is in the voice of professing subjects, including stars, trees, fish, birds, angels, rivers, choral directors, teachers, slaves, Indians, sacristans, and occasionally herself. This subjective slant takes the edge off statements, which, at least to the modern sensibility, seem exaggerated or overdrawn. Much of what is voiced in Sor Juana's devotional poetry, is done so either in praise or invocation, heightening the subjective coloring of the "content," while simultaneously lending emotional intensity and credibility to the text. The one voice she does not presume to know or to create is that of Mary herself, thereby avoiding another pitfall of pious writing—the bathos that inevitably accompanies such efforts. Whereas most women religious writers like María of Ágreda and Teresa of Ávila drew their authority from mystical experience, Sor Juana writes with the authority that comes from her intellectual and literary talents. Neither does she need to appeal to the mystical experience of the reader as a basis for understanding what she writes. Because she draws on both intellectual and on devotional traditions, her religious writing is open to the educated reason of the elite, as well as the imaginative intuitive understanding of the uneducated populace.

5

Bold Adventuress: Mary as a Model for Women

Clear the way for the entrance
of the bold adventuress
who undoes injustice,
who smashes insults . . .
Knight errant of the spheres
on a new adventure,
she finds the hidden treasure
sought by so many . . .

(OC 2:10-11)

Mary has long been proposed to the Catholic faithful as the model woman. Typically her virginity, obedience, humility, and silence have been extolled. One of the classical Marian enthusiasts whom Sor Juana read, as noted earlier, was Bernard of Clairvaux, whose fame as a devotee of Mary rests on a relatively small number of sermons which, through their intense fervor and the beauty of their language, had a broad and long lasting influence. In his homily for the feast of the Annunciation, which Sor Juana doubtless knew, he describes Mary as a timid virgin hidden away, locked in her room fleeing human company avoiding "conversation lest the silence of one given to prayer should be disturbed and the purity of one given to chastity be assailed."[1] Her motherhood is rather grudgingly admitted in contrast to the exaltation of her virginity. "What unique virginity.

Motherhood did not stain but honored it."[2] Humility, however, is unquestionably the highest virtue: "I dare say that without humility not even Mary's virginity would have been acceptable."[3] María of Ágreda, Sor Juana's Spanish contemporary, has Mary praise humility as "the firm foundation of all the wonders, which the Most High wrought in me . . . of all others, it is at the same time the most precious, the most delicate and perishable."[4]

Similar interpretations of Mary are to be found today. John Paul II's *Redemptoris Mater*, for example, though it does not portray Mary as hidden away in a room, does refer to her "hidden" and unassuming life as the "first of the 'little ones' of whom Jesus will say one day: 'Father . . . you have hidden these things from the wise and understanding'" (Mt 11:25). "Obedience in faith," rather than humility, is her "heroic" virtue.[5] Her glory as Mother is also due to her obedience to the word of God which she pondered and kept in her heart.

Recent reflection on Mary has raised questions about her image in view of the changing role of women today. In such works as Marina Warner's *Alone of All Her Sex*, a critical look at Mary as a means of domesticating women has begun to be systematically explored.[6] In *Under the Heel of Mary*, Nicholas Perry and Loreto Echeverría develop the theory that the Marian doctrine and the cultivation of Marian devotions have emerged in curious, nearly causal relationships, with political repression and reaction.[7] E. Johnson sees the Marian tradition as having "truncated the ideal of feminine fulfillment and wholeness."[8]

VIRGINITY

SOR JUANA ALSO appears to be aware of the dilemma presented to women with this model. Without expressly formulating her opposition to traditional understanding of virginity, humility, and obedience, she modifies them significantly in ways corresponding to feminists' critique of Mary as a symbol of what oppresses rather than liberates women. Sor Juana's attitude toward virginity is a critique of the double standard of application. Though virginity was technically a virtue praised in both men and women following the religious life, it was a necessary prerequisite for women marrying for the first time but not for men. In response to a reader from Peru whose admiration led him to recommend that she "return" as a man, Sor Juana comments dryly that if she is a woman, there is no one who can verify it. In Latin, she reminds him, the word *uxor* refers only to married women, the word *virgin* to both men and women. It is obvious that people consider her as a woman, but there is no one who can use her "as a woman" (OC 1:138). Implied, is that the call to virtue rests equally on men and women. Mary, yes, was a virgin but so was Jesus. Sor Juana has the anguished Mary viewing with "virginal eyes" the "virginal body" of her son exposed on the cross (OC 4:507). St. Joseph was also a virgin. In her *villancicos* for his feast, three of the poems consider his virginity.

> In fact, Joseph was doubly a virgin:
> Any intact virgin
> is only a virgin once
> but to be doubly virgin
> is alone the crown of Joseph.
> Any virgin keeps
> for herself her integrity
> but Joseph kept his own
> and that of his spouse.
> . . . . .
> O Virgin of all (male) virgins
> crowned holy king
> you offer a double sacrifice
> in one act of faith.

(OC 2:134–35)

The sixth poem for the feast develops a charming dialogue between Joseph and God about which of them demonstrated the greatest love (*fineza*). Among other things, Joseph argues that he agreed to renounce having descendants so that You [God] would have a Virgin for a Mother" (OC 2:136–37).

Joseph is also portrayed as having other virtues traditionally exalted in Mary. Like her, he was obedient to the voice of an angel (OC 2:136). To the question why have Mary married at all, Sor Juana adds a fifth of her own to the four of the tradition: Mary was married to Joseph to reward him for his virtue. He alone of all men was worthy to be called "father" by God. In this, Joseph can also be seen to parallel Mary who "alone of all women" was found worthy to be the Mother of God. The effect of this paralleling is not to diminish Mary by comparing her to Joseph, but rather to plead for the potential equality of the sexes in terms of their capacities for intellectual development (Sor Juana's point in her verses to the Peruvian admirer) and moral development (as in her poems for the feast of St. Joseph).

Sor Juana sees her own virginity not primarily in terms of sexual abstinence, but in terms of independence:

> What has pleased me most
> is to see that from here on
> I have only myself
> as my lineage.
>
> Isn't it something to know
> that I don't depend on anyone,
> that I die or live
> as it pleases me;
>
> To know I'm not the object of
> vulgar relations,
> nor do I need to be fatigued by relatives
> or bothered by godparents;
>
> To know that as only one of my species
> I don't need to bow to anyone
> since one is only obliged
> to love one's equal.

(OC 1:146)

Joseph also participates in Mary the dark one's race; at least in the minds of his African devotees. In possibly one of the earliest attempts to trace a genealogy for a black Jesus, Sor Juana has one of the characters in her celebration for the feast of St. Joseph proclaim that Señor San José could have been black. When another asks where would he get this lineage, the *Negro* answers, through the Queen of Sheba, who was the wife of King Solomon. Indeed the lineage of Jesus, traced through the line of Joseph in the Gospel of Matthew, includes the African queen (OC 2:143).[9]

PURITY

MARY'S PURITY IN Sor Juana's eyes, is her freedom from sin, both sins personally committed and original sin. From Augustine onwards, most theologians considered original sin to be connected to the impurity of the act of intercourse, and transmitted at the moment of conception. Mary represented the one exception to this rule by a special act of God in anticipation of the redemption from sin, through which her son would set right the broken relationships caused by the "eating of the forbidden fruit" in the garden. In Sor Juana's two sequences (1676 and 1689) for the feast of Mary's Conception, the most striking feature is her treatment of the first sin which led to the fall of humanity from grace. Whereas traditionally the sin was seen to be that of Eve, followed by Adam who was seduced by "the woman," Sor Juana, following the writings of Paul (Rom 5, 1 Cor 15), only refers to Adam's sin and almost never to the sin of Eve. She studiously avoids the common word play Ave/Eva. The Latin *ave* can mean not only "Hail," as in Ave Maria (Hail Mary), but also "bird." Ave read in reverse is Eva (Eve).[10] Even when Sor Juana plays with the word *ave*, she never uses it to refer to Eve. Though she refers to the instantaneous event of her sinless conception as "*en un Ave María*" as quickly as you can say a Hail Mary or, later in the same poem to Mary as "that queen of earth and Heaven . . . the bird (*ave*) of grace," she refrains from making any negative comparison to Eve (OC 2:20). Though the nun's avoidance of this figure may be seen as refusing to use a worn out metaphor, her consistent transformation of other typical expressions from Eve to Adam (OC 2:18–19), as in Mary as "*hija de Adán*," daughter of Adam, rather than daughter of Eve,[11] again indicate a conscious avoidance of attributing the entry of sin and death into the world to a woman (OC 2:18, OC 4:490–91).

HUMILITY

THOUGH SOR JUANA stresses Mary's humility, she does not identify it with obedience to higher authority, but rather associates it with power. In a poem for the Feast of the Assumption in 1690, using an image from the *Divine Comedy*, she compares Mary's humility to the point at the center of the earth, where Hell turns around and the way to Heaven is opened (OC 2:154, OC 4:516). She is "the queen of humility." The nun insists on Mary's agency and ability to describe herself, thereby working against the stereotypical picture of Mary as passive and silent. Building on Mary's phrase in the Magnificat, "the Lord has looked on his humble servant," she emphasizes that when Mary compares herself to dust (*humus*) it is not out of mortification, but as an appreciation of her value (OC 4:483). In one of her poems on the Incarnation, Sor Juana makes the same point, this time in Latin (OC 2:224). There, also, she uses the expression of Mary as humble "servant of the Lord" to set up a parallel between Mary, as the one who will conceive Christ, *the* servant of the Lord, and Jesus. The final chorus ends with a rousing "Vivat, Vivat, Vivat María!" recalling the shouts of triumph given a returning hero in classical Rome as well as the hosannas proclaimed by the enthusiastic crowd as Jesus entered Jerusalem (OC 2:224).

MARY'S LEADERSHIP

SOR JUANA MOVES beyond illustrating Mary's power to act and speak, to encouraging the faithful to experience Mary's speech. She does this in her *Devotional Exercises*. There, each day of the novena, after a meditation on some aspect of Mary's participation in creation, she advises her listeners to reflect on what she has said, and to try to imitate the particular virtue of Mary which has been the focus of the day's meditation. She further suggests that they pray a number of prayers to Mary. Instead of the Hail Mary, however, Sor Juana most often recommends praying the Magnificat (a much longer prayer) up to nine times. The Magnificat is the voice of Mary in the New Testament, whereas the "Hail Mary" begins with the voice of Elizabeth blessing Mary and the child she is carrying, and concludes with the voices of believing petitioners calling for Mary's help. Her emphasis on the Magnificat enables the participants in the novena to enter, in a meditative way, into the experience of Mary as speaking, rather than as silent.

Mary's activities are many and varied, as exemplified in the earliest of Sor Juana's *villancicos* (OC 2:3–17) for the feast of the Assumption 1676. They also demonstrate much of what is typical of the others: their energy, range of voices, and complexity of Marian imagery, and therefore merit more detailed consideration. An opening chorus summons the assembly to a debate between Earth and Heaven, who, on this feast, are vying for pre-eminence. Heaven argues his privilege based on the greater pleasure of Mary's ascending to triumph, over God's descending to suffer. Heaven offers Mary a crown of stars, whereas Earth gives Christ a crown of thorns. Earth counters that God left Heaven to seek the more beautiful dwelling of Mary's womb, and that Christ preferred the flesh, which he assumed on earth to the glory of Heaven. The disputation ends as the rejoicing community recognizes that both Mary's assumption as well as the kenosis of her son unite, rather than separate, Heaven and Earth who are then both called to come to celebrate with the refrain: "*Vengan, vengan, vengan!*" (OC 2:4).

The second poem, written in Latin and beginning with images of pregnancy and motherhood, stresses the sovereignty of Mary as the one who carried the Lord of Heaven and divine Word in her womb. As Christ's mother, she is presented as God's disciplinarian. The One before whom the heavens tremble was subject and obedient to her. Creation worships her: the moon kisses her virgin feet, the stars crown her, and the sun's rays bathe her in glory. Around her crowd the angelic hosts as Mary, *victrix* (the conqueror), ascends to heaven which, *as* she enters, is transformed into the bridal chamber of the triune God. In a second shift, the bridal chamber is transformed into a throne room in which Mary is crowned as Queen of Heaven, completing in the glory of her own person the glory of heaven. The heavenly chorus closes the poem with a question and answer: "Who is this, who like a green shoot (*virga*) rises from the desert more beautiful than the stars, the sun, and the moon? It is Mary!" (OC 2:5).

From the solemnity of Latin, Sor Juana moves back into Spanish for a series of playful, yet profound, comparisons in the ensuing five poems. In the first of these, Mary is presented as the most eminent theologian. As the sovereign doctor of the schools, from whom even the angels learn, she occupies the highest theological chair. Through participation in divine life at all different levels, Mary excels across the spectrum of required courses. As first of all creatures, she mastered all scientific knowledge. She cultivates theological topics. No one was more assiduous in the study of charity (*de Caritate*) than Mary. "Grace" (*de Gratia*) she knew even before her birth. "Incarnation" (*de Incarnatione*) she was able to study in herself, which gave her the best insight into "Trinity" (*de Trinitate*). Acclaimed the best candidate by students and professors on earth and in heaven, Mary is again cheered as victorious "in spite of Hell and its envy," this time as a new doctor of theology (OC 2:7).

The fourth poem praises Mary as heavenly choral director in an extended metaphor replete with punning on musical terminology of which my summary can only give a brief indication. From the low note of humility of the *Ecce ancilla* (Behold the handmaid of the Lord) to the high note of the "*Exaltata*" (hymn for the feast of the Assumption), Mary exhibits her musical expertise. In divine counterpoint, she is the most perfect. Beside her, the Judiths and Rebeccas of antiquity had minor parts. More beautiful than the music of the harp of Orpheus, which suspended the sufferings of the damned, is her music. The angelic choruses and the celebrating church accompany her with sonorous octaves, which finally merge into an eternal three part harmony.

Classical simplicity marks the style of the fifth poem. Mary is the beautiful shepherdess who, with one glance, wounds the heart of the divine shepherd. Combining baroque pastoral motifs with images from the Song of Songs, Mary is the divine bride, God is her eager solicitous lover. In the final chorus, the faithful, like shepherds, are called to run to the hilltop to see Mary rising to the heavens, robbing the village of its treasure.

The sacred *villancicos* included secular forms, not only of poetry, but also of music (OC 2:359–60). The sixth poem is a *jácara*, a song of thugs, ruffians, picaros, and wandering soldiers. Mary is "*la valiente de aventuras*," a female "knight-errant." She is dressed in resplendent armor: Her boots are like the moon, her helmet like stars, her shield glows with a light that illuminates Hell. Her motto: totally beautiful. In images reminiscent of St. George killing the dragon, Sor Juana shows Mary, the knight, breaking the spell of the cunning serpent. She rights the injustices done to the poor and liberates humanity, prisoners of original sin. All Hell trembles at the mention of her name. The "most beautiful warrior," she is the famous Paladin who conquered the Holy Land. She, knight errant of the spheres, found the hidden treasure sought by so many. It is only fitting she should not die like all others when she lived like no other.

The seventh section looks at Mary in terms of power of expression. She is the *rhetorica neuva* (new orator or rhetorician). Her eyes and her look are more eloquent than the rhetoric of Demosthenes and Cicero, the most eloquent orators of antiquity. As in her description of Mary as supreme choral director, in this section, Sor Juana uses technical terms, this time of classical rhetoric, in developing her metaphor. Mary's conception is an *exordium* (the beginning of a discourse), her life a narration, her death "confirmation" (confirming proof in an argument), her assumption the epilogue. She is the expert lawyer who persuades the judge to clemency. All her rhetoric can be reduced to the one Word.

In the last segment of the *villancicos*, for the Feast of the Assumption, Sor Juana gives voice to the common people who are Mary's enthusiastic followers by including the Spanish dialect of the black slaves and, as well as Nahautl. Traditionally, the last song was an *ensaladilla*, meaning medley, but also suggesting a tossed salad. It was intended to be humorous in order to wake people up at the end of the lengthy service (OC 2:362).

In the introductory stanza, the voices of the people present join the chorus of the angels, praying to their Señora to keep them together in peace and justice. Two *negros* are then introduced who have been moved by the festivities: one Heráclito, to tears and the other Demócrito, to admiration. In a dialogue in *negro* dialect, Demócrito tries to persuade Heráclito to join in singing the glorious queen.[12] Heráclito says he wants to cry from grief because once Mary ascends to heaven, all the blacks are left in darkness. Demócrito replies, "If she goes to heaven she will be happy there, dressed in silks, contemplating her son, and standing on a star." "Let me cry. She is going and leaving us with all the work!" (OC 2:16). This from Heráclito. Demócrito counters with enthusiasm, that she is always watching over the Church. They then agree to sing a song together in praise of this queen who is neither white, nor Spanish: "Doesn't she say, 'I am *morena* (dark or black) because the sun has shone upon me?'"[13] Though this comic pair may seem to be a conventional stereotype, their two names indicate the "melancholy" of their fates. As Octavio Paz, in another context, has explained, from the time of the Renaissance, the pair, Heraclitus and Democritus together, was seen as the prototype of the melancholy character, representing two reactions against it: tears and laughter.

Indians follow these, dancing a *tocotín*, and singing a solemn rhythmic chant in Nahuatl.[14] Like Heráclito, they also express their sorrow at the departure of their Mother, their *tonantzin*. The Indians fear their mother will forget them. But perhaps, when she is joyful in heaven, she will remember them. All those devoted to her could be then drawn upward, as on a rope. She could cause her son to think of them, reminding him of his drinking her milk when he was small. The entire eight part vespers ends on the note of petition of the Indians, who promise that, with the help of Mary, their mother, they will cast off their sins.[15]

MARY'S SUFFERING AS MEDIATON OF DIVINE GRACE

THOUGH FORMALLY LESS interesting than her *villancicos*, Sor Juana's *Ofrecimientos de los dolores* (Offerings for the Sorrows of Mary) merits closer examination. It is one of two prose works mentioned in her defense of her intellectual life as being published with her permission. It consists of short meditations of less than one hundred fifty words. Each one is designed to set the theme for a decade of the Rosary and lead the believer into a deeper appreciation of and identification with an aspect of the passion of Jesus through the vision or viewpoint of Mary, his mother. Each day's meditation has three parts. The first invokes Mary. The second is the offering proper: praying ten "Hail Marys" and one "Our Father" in view of the particular suffering described as the subject of the meditation. The third is a plea for help, generally to persevere on the path of virtue.

The various stages of Jesus' passion—being scourged, taunted, stumbling under the weight of the cross, nailed on the cross—are typical of the piety of the seventeenth century and well represented in Mexican devotional art. The image of his suffering Mother, whose anguish was most often represented by a sword piercing her heart, is a-typical of Sor Juana's treatment of Mary which stresses the grace, energy, joy and glory of Mary, the Mother of God, the Spouse of the Almighty. In *Offerings*, Mary is the suffering mother before the naked and mutilated body of her son. A tradition going back as far as the twelfth century, which sought a parallel in the life of Mary which would correspond to Christ's passion, devotion to the sorrows of Mary, was strengthened in the seventeenth century, when permission was given by Pope Paul V (1605–21) to set up confraternities dedicated to her "seven sorrows." While Sor Juana retains the traditional point of view, paralleling Mary's emotional calvary with Christ's physical suffering, as a woman writing the woman's point of view, she again brings in accents which prefigure contemporary feminist concerns.

Sor Juana's portrayal of the "earthly" Mary, in the *Offerings*, concentrates on paralleling the most powerful function attributed to her son, that of his redemption of the sins of humanity through his suffering. Mary's own suffering during her son's passion is the reason she can be invoked to help the faithful to repent and/or persevere in virtue. Here, Sor Juana's meditations focus primarily on the redemptive dynamic of Mary as the suffering mother and secondarily on the actual suffering of Jesus who dies in the sixth of the fifteen meditations. Mary suffers seeing her son nailed to the cross. Her tender heart bleeds as the cross is raised and the blood of the wounds of Christ flows from his hands and feet. She suffers abandonment when her son gives her into the care of his disciple John. More bitter than the bitter herbs Jesus is offered to drink, is the cup of bitterness she drinks at the sight. Unspeakable suffering, like an atrocious knife, penetrates her soul as she sees her son incline his head and die. She suffers alone under the cross where her dead son hangs, and hers is the suffering heart as the centurion's lance pierces the heart of the dead Jesus. As she holds his body, she mourns the beauty of his living body, the "reflection of all beauty," which she took in her arms to nurse and which she saw expire on the arms of the cross. She suffers the final deprivation of his presence as he is lowered into the "cold grave," the last enclosure of his body contrasting cruelly to its first enclosure, her "warm womb."

The last four offerings serve to extend Mary's suffering to the suffering of all in danger of "eternal death": Those who die without baptism, heretics, reprobate Christians, and finally, to her suffering from the sins of the just. Mary's intercession is invoked in order to persuade her son to change the fate of those destined for eternal death so that, in the case of the gentiles, the "light of the Gospel will reach the peoples in the darkness . . ."; so that "the heretics will be rescued from the mouth of the wolf and reconciled with the Church militant, (and) will enjoy the church triumphant (in eternity)"; so that those Christians in mortal sin will repent before the hour of their death. Through Mary's intercession mercy will reign, theoretically implied, for all.

Throughout the *Offerings,* contemplation of Mary's suffering serves to grace the petitioner. Believers are urged to be open to the message of the wounds of Mary and Jesus, "suffered for our love; so that, corresponding as we ought to their gracious benefits," the faithful will serve Christ and suffer willingly for the benefit of others (OC 4:512). Each suffering of Jesus inspires a corresponding virtue in the petitioner. Thus, the pain in Mary's heart when she heard Jesus' cry of abandonment corresponds to the petition not to abandon the faithful in their hour of death; Mary's anguished witness to the bitter cup of vinegar offered to her thirsting son is petitioned to inspire patience in the bitterness of the mortifications of this life. Her suffering at the moment of the death of her son is called upon to give them strength and courage to die to the things of this world. And so on. Within this stylized, nearly formulaic structure, Sor Juana manages to evoke another strength of Mary's, her strength to suffer for the good of all humankind. It is through her freely bestowed gift of suffering, as well as that of her son, that the gates of eternal life are opened.[16]

Images associated with women's bodies (blood flow, penetration, and physical violation) are especially apparent in her description of Jesus' wounds and Mary's response to the sight of them. The entire sequence of the meditations opens with Mary arriving tired and weeping at Golgotha to see the cross being lifted from the shoulders of Jesus, his clothes torn off his body, "taking with them pieces of his mutilated flesh," leaving "his virginal body" exposed to the eyes of the multitude. Mary's suffering at this moment crystallizes in the "unspeakable shame" which suffuses her face when her "virginal eyes" see him exposed and naked. Mary is asked to intercede with God so that "the outrages and wounds of our sins and the nakedness (*desnudez*) of our merits are covered and substituted" by the merits of Mary's tears. By mentioning Jesus and Mary's virginity, Sor Juana suggests similarity rather than difference, equality rather than subordination.

CRITIQUE OF CLERICAL POWER

SOR JUANA'S TREATMENT of Mary, which presents her in images replete with activity (adventuress, teacher, choral director, etc.), contrasts with her treatment of the "prince of apostles," Peter. Elizabeth Johnson has pointed out that "the lack of Mary of Nazareth's public involvement has led some to make the distinction between Mary as the model of the believing disciple and Peter as the model of the apostolic disciple, a distinction which again turns the Marian symbol into a potential tool of patriarchial power."[17] Sor Juana also avoids this trap. What today's feminist theologians would call the critique of patriarchy, can be found in Sor Juana's satirical presentation of figures representing authorities and institutions such as the university and the church.[18] We can see this principally in her *loas* and her *villancicos*, where students engage in self-conscious debate, and sacristans mangle their Latin. George Tavard has recognized this: "Sacristans (representing the all-male clergy) and scholars (the all-male university) are often the butt of Juana's [*sic*] not so innocent jokes!"[19] Her spirit and sense of fun, as well as her command of the *villancico*, allow her space for the critique of existing power structures, including the foundational figure of Peter. Perhaps the most audacious of these dates from the early period of her writing. In 1677 for the feast of St. Peter Sor Juana elaborates scriptural passages which emphasize his humiliations, and relativize his authority—the reverse dynamic of her Marian songs. Her first song presents a choir of angels singing, what is, in effect, an apology for her method of not stressing Peter's titles of glory, such as head of the church militant, or even martyr: "The name that Christ gave him was the one that has the greatest value and nobility: Peter, the rock."

The second song begins with the joyful summoning of children to school. In a touch typical of Sor Juana's feminist awareness, the "first teacher" in the mosaic of songs composed to honor Peter, the founder of the "teaching magisterium," is an elementary school teacher, a role often (as in Sor Juana's own life) occupied by a woman. The teacher is dictating to children on their slates the "different types of print" in which they can write about Peter: the "romanilla," because he is from Rome, "liberal," because he liberates the gates of heaven, not "bastard," because he makes of bastards "sons and daughters of the church," etc.[20] (OC 2:46). Though joyous in tone, the text takes on darker implications when the pupils are urged to "conserve the purity" of their writing, watching every comma, so as not to be accused of heresy.

The third segment shows Peter as the great bookkeeper recording sins, and erasing those forgiven. At the same time, the association with the church and money is not far below the surface, especially in its final chorus: "Divine accountant, Count, Count, Count, and erase our debts from your book. And, since you have such skill in accounting, multiplying, adding, dividing, and subtracting, multiply graces and divide punishments" (OC 2:48). A more dignified Latin hymn follows in which the "second Rome" is compared to the ancient Roman empire. *Villancico* five takes us back to the schoolroom, this time Peter is a dimwitted teacher of Latin grammar and poetry. The sixth poem claims to be presenting a syllogism in which Peter, as a poor logician (*mal lógico*), though he knew that Jesus was "the Christ, the Son of the living God," denied knowing him in the courtyard of the high priest. Peter's "teacher," in this scene, is the maidservant who recognizes "the truth," that is, that he *is* one of Jesus' disciples (OC 2:53).

In her seventh poem, Sor Juana features Peter as the "fencing master," based on the scene in the Garden of Gesthemane in which Peter cuts off the ear of Malchus, the servant of the High Priest. Numerous technical references to slashing and thrusting rob the figure of Peter of any shred of majesty he might have left. We are left wondering how this text passed official censorship. One reason may be that the Spanish church's relationship to Rome was more ambivalent than is commonly thought. The Spanish Inquisition was set up independently of Rome, and was, essentially, an arm of the state.

Another reason may be that a humorless reader would have missed the mocking tone, or that the possibility of a serious point being made in a musical text was outside the horizon of the readers. Her less than reverential treatment has been the cause of astonishment from numerous interpreters, including editor Méndez Plancarte, and more recently George Tavard, who prefers to select from the *villancicos* "attributed" to her those that show proper reverence to the "prince of the apostles," the model for the papacy.

Sor Juana even oversteps, at least in imagination, the prohibition of women's ordination. Here again, the light tone of the *villancicos* allow her explicitly, though hypothetically, to assume the voice of "preacher" in the twentieth poem of the cycle for the dedication of a church to Bernard of Clairvaux. In the first stanza:

> The Church, Bernard, and Mary,
> It would be a good occasion
> to bring them into concert
> if I were a preacher.
> But no, no, no, no:
> I'm not cut of such fine cloth.
> But supposing that I were,
> what things would I say
> moving from text to text
> searching for connections?
> But No, no, no, no:
> I'm not cut of such fine cloth . . .
>
> (OC 2:202–3)

In the succeeding three stanzas, she proceeds to say what she would say "if she were a preacher" each time ending with the refrain, "No, no, no, no: I'm not cut of such fine cloth." She in fact, delivers such a sermon, all the while, denying she is doing so. The reaction of Sor Juana's admiring editor, a priest himself, Méndez-Plancarte is instructive. He initially calls her hypothetical example a "*graciosa hipótetis*," which can mean graceful but, also, funny or amusing, commenting that "certainly she would have been magnificent." He then admits that she would have been capable of developing a sermon for the occasion. Finally, he even concedes that she did preach in her theological prose, hastily qualifying that she did it "in written form and privately" (OC 2:451).

6

On the Benefits of Christ's Love: <u>Athenagoric Letter</u>

Muy señor mío: *From the babbling of a conversation in which you graciously granted me much keenness and liveliness of spirit, was born in you the desire to see some of that discourse in written form which I, there, made spontaneously concerning the sermons of an excellent orator* . . .

> Opening lines of
> *Athenagoric Letter*
> (OC 4:412)

THE 1690 PUBLICATION of *Athenagoric Letter* (Letter Worthy of Athena), a critique of a sermon of the Portuguese Jesuit, Antonio Vieira, resulted in Sor Juana's writing her most acclaimed prose work, *Respuesta a Sor Philotea de la Cruz* (Response to Sor Philotea de la Cruz). Published without her permission, it was prefaced by an admonishing letter from the bishop of Puebla, Fernández de Santa Cruz, under the pseudonym Sor Philotea de la Cruz. Constance Montross has shown that the *Letter* has the structure of a classical sermon,[1] and as Jean Franco has demonstrated, with this work Sor Juana is de facto "trespassing in the pulpit."[2] Sor Juana's insistence on the convent parlor as the (severely restricted) forum of her intended critique of Vieira, as well as her description of the genesis of her ideas as trivial (the chatter of a social gathering), indicate her desire to situate herself within a frame of discourse permitted to women.

THE SERMON WAS a popular and very public form of discourse which could often count on audiences of thousands, far beyond that of many plays.[3] When published, a sermon could reach a diverse and extended audience, becoming a forum through which theological discussion entered broad public debate and even extended into the international arena. In 1666, the English consul at Lisbon characterized Vieira as "a Jesuit eminent for his preaching, his sermons being bought up as fast as they are printed, and sent for out of all parts of Spain, Italy, and France."[4]

As Luso-Brazilian scholar Robert Ricard has observed, *Athenagoric Letter* brought together two of the most extraordinary figures in colonial literature: "the Portuguese preacher António Vieira and the Mexican poet Sor Juana Inés de la Cruz."[5] Vieira's (1608–97) long and eventful life was nearing its end among the Indians in Brazil at the time of the publication of the *Letter*. An acclaimed preacher at the court of John IV of Portugal, he had defended the rights of Indians and Jewish converts and been censured by the Roman Inquisition. He had also been a confessor to Christina, queen of Sweden, before returning to Brazil in 1680 Though they certainly never met, and most probably Vieira never read, perhaps never even heard of Sor Juana's *Letter*, one person may have known both of them: Archbishop Aguiar Y Seijas. By 1690, when Sor Juana wrote her critique, several volumes of Vieira's sermons which had been translated into Spanish and published in Madrid were dedicated to Francisco Aguiar y Seijas, then archbishop of Mexico; an indication of a possible connection between the two. Scholars presume that Sor Juana had access to Vieira's sermon in one of these translations.[6]

Vieira's and Sor Juana's lives offer interesting parallels, and it is tempting to speculate that Sor Juana sensed a kindred spirit in the flamboyant, even arrogant, Vieira in spite of differences of style and emphasis. Indeed, the nun indicates as much in her opening words of praise, which need not be read as formulaic or necessarily ironic, when she writes that, Vieira like herself was "a daughter," no less than he was implicitly a son, of "sacred religion" (OC 4:413). Like Sor Juana, he identified with the Americas, maintaining an active interest in Brazilian politics even during his years in Portugal. Though born in Portugal, he went to Brazil at the age of six in 1614. There he entered the Jesuit order (1623), returning to Portugal only in 1641. Both writers had strong ties to court life: Vieira as royal preacher from 1644 to 1662 at the Portuguese court,[7] and as confessor to Queen Christina of Sweden. Sor Juana's connections to the viceregal court in Mexico have already been discussed. Both the Jesuit and the nun had international reputations in their lifetimes. Even the language used to describe them is similar. Sor Juana had been entitled variously the "Mexican phoenix" and "empress of the language," as was Vieira the "Lusitanian (Portuguese) phoenix" and "emperor of the Portuguese tongue."[8]

LETTER WORTHY OF ATHENA[9]

THE "SCHOLASTIC" MODE of argumentation of the *Athenagoric Letter* baffles modern interpreters. Paz has characterized both Vieira's and Sor Juana's work as "vain subtlety and an empty ingenuity . . ."[10] However, Sor Juana's method delighted many of her contemporaries in Spain at the 1692 publication of the second volume of her collected works, which Paz has termed as "the most important volume . . . the most varied . . . the richest . . . her best work."[11] There the *Letter,* with Sor Juana's own title, *Critique of a Sermon,* is given the first place in the volume. In one of the most complimentary of the many encomiums of the official censors, there is a play on the name given Vieira's sermon, the *Mandato.* (A reference to Christ's command at the last supper to love as he loved.) Cristoval Bañes de Salceda wrote on July 15, 1691 near the end of his "Censura": "Not only do I give permission (*licencia*) but I command (*mandato*) that this be printed."

Furthermore, Paz's complaint that both Vieira's sermon and Sor Juana's *Letter* are not applied "to any real object" and are devoid of "authentic religious sentiment" fails to see beneath the rhetorical superstructure. Vieira wrote his sermon for the mass of Holy Thursday to be preached at the Court of John IV of Portugal. The prescribed gospel text was from John 13 where Jesus washes the feet of his disciples during the night of his last meal with them and commands them to do the same. Furthermore, the seemingly academic or obscure topic, which is the greatest *fineza* (demonstration of love) of Christ, moves Vieira and, subsequently, Sor Juana to consider other related issues: the meaning and nature of the death and suffering of Christ and consequently human suffering and death; the character of Christ's presence in the Eucharist; and the relationship between love of God and love of neighbor.

RHETORIC AND LOGIC

VIEIRA'S SERMON IS the work of a master preacher and rhetorician. In the rhetorical structure of the sermon, his claim to better the opinions of the fathers, which Sor Juana uses to emphasize her own modesty, is part of an exhortation to his listeners to be bold and passionate in their speaking about the love of God, and in their praise of God. He insists that any statement about God's love pales in comparison with its reality, and modesty is not appropriate here. Christ suffers more today from lukewarm speech ("our tepid tongues") about him than from the "cruelty of the hands" which crucified him. The Jesuit begs God for help in his praise, and completes his introduction by saying that one of God's greatest *finezas* is God's suffering caused by human beings saying so little of him in his presence.[12]

Vieira begins by justifying his choice of the *finezas* as a topic. Just as God, in the order of creation, manifested his power to the utmost on the last day, so in the order of redemption, Christ reserved the best demonstration of his love for the last day with his disciples. Though everything Christ did on the last day of his life would have heightened significance, Vieira says his own curiosity and the devotion of his audience moves him to inquire which of the demonstrations of the last day is the "greatest." He finds his answer in Christ's admonishment to his disciples "to wash one another's feet" as he has washed theirs. This act is paradigmatic for the relationship of God to humanity, which, as Christ revealed, moves beyond justice to love, making the rain to fall on just and unjust alike without regard for merits or offenses. Vieira reminds those who see this as unfair that, beginning with his incarnation, Christ took the form of the most lowly "the slave". With the sweat of his brow, he earned his bread, and as a slave, he washed the feet of his disciples. As a slave, he was sold by Judas into the hands of his enemies. Furthermore, he died for all, including the unjust, the impious.

Approximately the concluding fourth of the sermon is an elaborate plea to his hearers to love one another, to love those who are undeserving, to love their enemies, to go beyond the *rational* love, which only loves those who love us in return, to the love of enemies or non-Christians, because of Christ's example. Occurring almost every ten words in this last section, the word *love*, like an incantation, urges his Christian audience to love one another face to face. Even his enemies, Christ could call friends—as he addressed

Judas when he came to betray him: "Friend, why have you come?" (Mt 26:50). In a final point, Vieira reminds them that even such enemies of Jesus as Herod and Pilate were inspired to become friends "on this day" after their contact with Jesus. Those present should use the occasion to forgive and befriend each other.

If the word *love* resounds like a mantra in Vieira's sermon, the word *proof* hammers out the structure of Sor Juana's *Letter*. While praising the beauty of the "edifice" Vieira has built, she comments that the beauty of a structure is more apparent when its foundation is weak, thereby implying that the decoration of rhetoric is likely to conceal a weak foundation rather than being there to ornament a strong line. Once beyond the opening apology, what she herself constructs is Vieira's position reduced to a series of logical propositions explicitly described as *proofs*. Sor Juana's analysis of Vieira's position and her own counter arguments maintain a syllogistic structure throughout the *Letter*. She shows that she is *conscious* of presenting his ideas in a strikingly different manner when she writes:

> These are in substance his reasons and proofs, although so as not to linger, or to take up more space, I have reduced them to the coarseness of my style, where they lose not a little of their energy and sharpness. It will be necessary to do this for the rest of his argument (OC 4:415.126–30).

In addition to her recasting Vieira's arguments into syllogistic forms, she also raises numerous objections to them on the basis of formal logic. For example, Vieira argues that the greatest *fineza* of Christ is not, as Thomas Aquinas maintained, becoming present in the sacrament of the Eucharist, but "suffering" from not "seeing" his beloved followers, because of being deprived of the use of his senses beneath the accidents of bread and wine. Sor Juana objects, saying Thomas Aquinas's example was a general one, and Vieira's a subset of it. As such, it could not be considered to contradict the general principle. Vieira has committed the error of arguing against a major premise with a minor one, an error in formal logic. Similarly, she faults him for the logical error of maintaining that the cause is greater than the resulting effect, when he claims, against John Chrysostom, that Christ's *motive* in washing the feet of his enemy Judas was the greater *fineza*, not his actual washing of all his disciples. Sor Juana contends that, though Christ's motive is not distinct from the effect, it cannot be *demonstrated* because the immensity of the mind of God cannot be reduced to one motive. Christ's prostrating himself at his disciples' feet, was the humbling of that "Immense Majesty at the feet of humanity" (OC 4:422.430–31), a symbolic reminder of the miracle of the Incarnation which was intended to stimulate our desire for the eternal rewards. Bathing Judas' feet only exaggerated the length to which God will go to solicit the *conversion* of Judas. Another example from the "order of redemption" underscores her point: For the conversion of humanity, God sent His only Son. The effect, the sending of the Son, proves the motivation, i.e., God so loved the world. Finally, for Sor Juana, it is better to leave closer speculation about God's motivation under a veil of silence because of its ultimate inscrutability.

EMOTION VS. REASON

ANOTHER STRIKING CONTRAST in the work of nun and priest is in their approach to emotion. Vieira emphasizes the emotions; his own, his listeners', and those of Christ. His first criterion for measuring the degree of love shown by Christ is an emotional one: the degree of suffering involved. Which caused Christ more suffering, his loss of life, or his loss of fellowship? His option for loss of fellowship as the greatest suffering indicates a choice of the relational over the ontological. "The loving Lord suffered more from leaving those He loved than from leaving His very life . . . more the loss of company than the destruction of His essence."[13] His highlighting emotion runs parallel with his focus on the body and the importance of physical presence. The friendship of Christ with his disciples implies a physical presence of the disciples and Christ to each other. Mary Magdalene suffered more at the empty tomb than under the cross when Christ died, because she discovered the absence of Jesus' body. On the cross, his body was still present to her. Again, when considering the manner of Christ's presence in the Eucharist, a similar emphasis on concrete physicality is evident. Not only do believers, such as Mary Magdalene, long for the physical presence which the Eucharist embodies, but Christ himself longs to be physically present to his disciples. Thus when Vieira maintains that Christ's greatest *fineza* in the Eucharist is "His being present without seeing those He loves," he means it in a very realistic manner: Being present

under the "accidents" of bread and wine, Christ does not have th
use of his senses, and therefore, cannot "see" his disciples.[14]

Sor Juana's insistence on her "reasonableness" in her opening
strategies serves not only to counter typical stereotyping of women
as "emotional," but is also representative of her conviction that the
intellect is, as she describes it, "a free power which agrees or dis-
agrees according to what it judges to be or not to be the truth"
(OC 4:413.41–44). Using her logical skills to good advantage she
makes points against the Jesuit's contention that Christ's suffering
of absence was a greater demonstration of his love than his death.
Absence itself may be temporary. Death is permanent absence of
the physical presence of the beloved and, therefore, is more painful,
and as such, according to Vieira's own criteria, more of a demonstration of Christ's love than his mere absence. Here again, the
manner of Sor Juana's response can be seen to represent the shift to
a more empirical method, investigating causes rather than appealing
to the power of empathy. When refuting the example of Mary Magdalene's tears at the empty tomb, she does it on the basis of an
analysis of the meaning of tears. The mere existence of tears, she
observes, does not prove either sorrow or joy since they can be a
response to great pleasure or great pain. She also draws on the psy-
chology of tears, which held that in great sorrow,, the vital forces
are gathered around the heart, suspending other actions and move-
ments. Only when the initial shock has abated are they released in a
flood of tears (OC 4:419.280–97).

Whereas Vieira emphasizes Christ's physical presence and his
suffering, Sor Juana tends to stress Christ's majesty and his difference from the rest of humanity. The aspect of Christ's suffering
which most interests her is metaphysical rather than physical: In
death his surrendering of his very being was the greatest imaginable
deprivation. Christ became incarnate, in "the flesh," but for Sor
Juana it is not in the sinful flesh of "humanity," but in the most
pure flesh of "His mother" (OC 4:417.231–33). This option also
leads her to the conclusion that Christ was not tempted in the same
way as other human beings because he was born of the Virgin
Mary, through miraculous conception, and could not be tempted
except by "suggestion," an extrinsic temptation which would not
really touch his inner core. Having neither the struggle nor the risk,
he could not demonstrate his love by resisting sin, nor fear the risk
of sinning" (OC 4:429.708–10).

Correspondences

Vieira may have been indulging in anachronistic thinking by even proposing that the issue of the *finezas* was present in the work of the three traditional authorities—Augustine, Aquinas, and John Chrysostom.[15] Neither Vieira nor Sor Juana cite specific works of any of the three authors mentioned, though they do cite other works.[16] Vieira merely states the "opinion" of each of the fathers in a phrase or sentence and then begins to present his own counter position. Similarly, Sor Juana's "arguing with" each of the fathers does not mean that the reasons she gives for supporting their respective positions are theirs. Thus, her arguing "with" Augustine really means she agrees with the received interpretation of him on the issue, i.e., that the greatest demonstration of Christ's love was his death.

The word *fineza* for Sor Juana does not designate the feeling or condition of *love* as an interior act.[17] Rather, *finezas* are the exterior demonstrative signs and actions of the lover which have love as their cause (OC 4:423.473–75). Though she does not quote Vieira, she is clearly taking issue with his understanding of *fineza*, which in effect does identify it with interior motivation. He calls it *amor fino*, which seeks neither cause nor fruit[18] and is characterized by a "degree of sensitivity or delicacy of love (*fineza*) which gives equal favors to those who are unequal in terms of their merits."[19] Consequently, the highest degree of love is not without a touch of pain. Thus the Jesuit ranks David's love for Saul, who betrayed him, above his love for Jonathan his friend; Jesus' love for Judas, above His love for the "beloved disciple" John. *Fineza* is "strong and delicate."[20] In general, Vieira measures the degree of love of Christ by the intensity of Christ's feelings as shown above.[21]

After defining the value of a particular *fineza* as deriving from both what it costs the donor and from the benefits it brings to the recipient, Sor Juana places her argument within the context of Christ's dual nature, divine and human. Accordingly, whereas the demonstrations of God's divine power, such as God's creating and sustaining life, are all of great benefit to humanity, they cannot be said to cost God anything because of God's infinite power to do these things. Even the Incarnation, a greater *miracle* than Christ's death, is not as great a demonstration of his love because it proceeds without cost to the donor. Constance Montross argues that inconsistencies in Sor Juana's counter arguments result from her initial attempt to *define* the Incarnation as a miracle *rather than* a *fineza*

(OC 4:416.188–92). In fact, Sor Juana *distinguishes* between the Incarnation as miracle, and the Incarnation as *fineza*. As a miracle, it is only something God can give due to God's omnipotence, and, therefore, only participates in one side of the *perfect* demonstration of love, that of benefit to the recipient. It lacks the criterion of effort of the donor.[22] Not so Christ's death which, in an unspoken appropriation of Thomistic anthropology, Sor Juana conceives of as the sundering of the unity of the human person. In his death, that unity of body and soul "which made Him Christ" was dissolved, with the ironic result that, as a human, he could do what as God he could not: give up his being (OC 4:417). Furthermore, from the Aristotelian/Thomistic conception of final causality, which sees the goal toward which an activity is directed as more important than the action of progressing toward the goal, Christ's death can be seen as his greatest gift. Since God became incarnate in Christ in order to die for humanity, the Incarnation was the necessary condition for Christ's death, and consequently, dying the greatest *fineza*.

As part of her logic, Sor Juana incorporates concepts and examples indicative of her interest in language, playing on various meanings of *word* which emphasize the dual aspects of Christ's nature. Thus she argues that, as Word of God incarnate, Christ overcame the infinite distance between God and humanity, but his own words at the last supper and on the cross reveal that his death, which "overcame the limited distance between humanity and death," was more important. At his last meal with his disciples, he urges them to commemorate his death (1 Cor 11:24), not his incarnation. On the cross, he indicates the supreme accomplishment of his death with the words: "*Consummatum est*" (It is accomplished) (John 19:30). Similarly, she refers to Christ's authoritative words, "Do this in memory of Me," as an indication of his valuing the Eucharist as a memorial of his death.

In a second supporting argument, Sor Juana compares Christ to a (human) lover. A lover wants what he considers most important about his love to be remembered. Christ tells his beloved disciples to remember his death, she writes, which is not only the greatest *fineza* but is the summary of all *finezas*. It presupposes the benefits rendered to humanity through his incarnation, restores humanity to its primary state of grace, and also sustains humanity in the life of grace through his body and blood in the Eucharist (OC 4:417).

The second possible *fineza*, which Vieira chooses to consider, again reflects the Holy Thursday liturgy that commemorates the institution of the Eucharist. Against Thomas Aquinas, who, according to Vieira, argued that the greatest *fineza* was Christ's abiding presence in the Eucharist, the Jesuit argues that the epitome of Christ's love was demonstrated not so much in the presence itself, but in its *paradoxical nature*. Following a logic which would see Christ's physical presence as limited in its identity with the bread and wine, he argues that Christ, in the Eucharistic elements of bread and wine, would be deprived of "His five senses," and, therefore, of his ability to be "sensually" present to his disciples. As a result, this suffering of sensual deprivation is the aspect of his Eucharistic presence that shows the most love.

Sor Juana's basic criticism of this argument is that it is overly subtle, since Thomas Aquinas's understanding of the Eucharistic presence included the aspect of the deprivation of senses, which Vieira saw as "the greatest." However, if the issue at hand were which of the *aspects* of Christ's presence in the Eucharist demonstrated the greatest love, she opts for a presence, rather than an absence: "Christ's being present to the offenses of His enemies is a better example of His love than His suffering the absence of physical 'experience' of His disciples in His Eucharistic presence." She continues: "Not to see what gives pleasure is painful, but it is more painful to see what causes displeasure or hurt" (OC 4:421.394–95). The patriarch Jacob demonstrated the validity of this principle when he did not punish his sons, who were responsible for the enslavement of their brother Joseph, and who, thereby, deprived him of the presence of his beloved son, but did punish his son Ruben who had "violated his bed" and, therefore, his honor, an offense that would be constantly present.

The third aspect of the Holy Thursday gospel which Vieira brings before his listeners is the scene in which Christ washes the feet of his disciples. John Chrysostom argued that this *action* of Christ was the greatest *fineza*, but Vieira insists his *motivation* in washing them is of a higher order. Again, Sor Juana says that John Chrysostom would have intended to include the motive in the act, since motive and act like cause and effect are inseparable. The gesture *reveals* the interior motivation and the degree to which Christ would go to solicit the conversion of his disciples, even of Judas.

When Sor Juana has finished her defense of "the fathers," she moves to critique what she calls the weakest point of his argument, the "Achilles heel of his sermon": his view that Christ does not want our love in response to his, but desires only that we love one another. She interprets the Jesuit as maintaining it is Christ's preference that our experience of his love motivate us to love our neighbor, rather than increase our love for him. Thus the highest love is "love without corresponding love," or love without reciprocity. It is not immediately clear why she insists on this point, especially since Vieira never explicitly makes it, though it can be inferred from his *emphasis* on the love Christ wishes his disciples to show to one another.

Be that as it may, Sor Juana again marshals a series of scriptural examples which "prove" that God not only *desires* human response (reciprocity), but *commands* it (OC 4:424.510–667). Repeatedly, she insists that love of God comes before love of neighbor. (1) God commands that we love our neighbor because God commands it. (2) Love of Christ goes beyond all other loving relationships, such as parents, spouses, friends. "The one who loves father or mother more than Me is not worthy of Me." (3) Though God commands we love our neighbors as ourselves, Christ demands that those wanting to follow him deny their very selves. (4) Love of Christ will cause stress and strife, "war to the death and fire." "I have not come to bring peace but the sword."

After her extensive counterarguments which have the effect of radicalizing the Jesuit's position to one which maintains that God is *indifferent* to human response (OC 4:428.674), she then proceeds to ask if there are *finezas* which Christ omits doing for us because of his immense love for us. Yes, there are. In fact, there are demonstrations of love that the faithful can do for Christ which he cannot do for them, such as resist temptations "by combatting our nature which is inclined to evil"(OC 4:429.681–83). Furthermore, to renounce correspondence for Christ would not be really giving up anything—by seeking love without reciprocity—because nothing would be added to *his* well-being by our returning his love. The true *fineza* of Christ is that he asks for our love even though he has no need of it (OC 4:430.745–48). Moreover, he wishes it for our good, not for his.

In fact, in his text, Vieira is more nuanced here than Sor Juana's rendering of him would give us to believe.[23] He sees love and corresponding response as two inherently reciprocal acts, one always mirroring the other. God's love, however, he writes, goes beyond the rational order which sees love in terms of equal exchange: You pay me what you owe me.[24] God turns this natural order around, desiring that we show our love of God by loving our neighbors, including our enemies. In fact, it is not possible for humans to make good the infinite debt they owe to God.

God's Greatest Fineza

In the final section of the *Letter*, Sor Juana moves from "using the fathers" against Vieira to explicitly presenting her own opinion. Her conversation partner in the convent parlor had also requested that she commit to writing her own opinion of the greatest demonstrations of *divine* love, as opposed to the final demonstration of the love of Christ at the end of his life. (This, she is careful to say, was not part of Vieira's sermon, but another topic.) The logic of her argument is simple: Given God's desire to communicate infinite goodness and love to all creatures, and God's omnipotence which can effect the perfect realization of God's will, the greatest demonstration of God's love is to withhold benefits because of humanity's demonstrable ingratitude toward such generosity. As the Bible shows time and again, we are not, in fact, capable of appropriately responding to such generosity. The people of Nazareth who enjoyed Christ's presence were the least receptive of his message, taunting and maligning him. Christ refused to work miracles there because it would only have increased their ingratitude. In the Old Testament, God regrets having created the world and all that it contains because of the corruption of humanity. The gift of life itself was not appreciated. Even illness and reverses of fortune should be seen in this light. If we had everything we desired, we would have no basis of comparison to be grateful for our good fortune.

Indirectly, Sor Juana is answering the classical question: "Why, if God is all good and all powerful, is there suffering in the world?" Suffering and misfortune are examples of God's deliberate noninterference in human affairs for two reasons: to spare us the sin of ingratitude; and to give us space to turn negative benefits into positive ones. Negative benefits fit another qualification of *fineza* elaborated in the preceding section: it must cost the lover effort and bring benefits for the beloved. Because it is God's nature to be generous, loving, and powerful, God's withholding benefits costs God more than giving benefits, as a result, this is the greatest demonstration of love (OC 4:436.985–98). What results is a dialectical view of divine love which is able to encompass what seems negative, such as hurt (punishment) and deficiency (withholding). "Let us be thankful for and ponder this excellence of divine love in which rewarding is a benefit, punishing a benefit, and the suspension of benefits the greatest benefit, and the lack of *fineza* the greatest *fineza*" (OC 4:439.1095–98).

Though the differences of "atmosphere" of Vieira's *Mandato Sermon* and Sor Juana's *Athenagoric Letter* may be due in part to a more general cultural shift in patterns of thinking, both authors escape stereotyping. Sor Juana, as a poet, breaks out of the rationalistic straitjacket which some have seen as characterizing emerging modernity,[25] and conversely, Vieira's writing can be read as an example of Aristotelian/Thomistic logic.[26] Furthermore, in spite of their differing accents, both Vieira and Sor Juana see God's love as paradigmatic of human love. The Jesuit stresses aspects of the Holy Thursday gospel text which highlight Christ in the role of servant or slave, a dialectical inversion of the expected relationship of the powerful (God) to the powerless (humanity). Christ's final demonstration of love, which culminates the kenosis of the Incarnation, is to "take on human nature in the lowliest stage of fortune, that of the slave".[27] Christ, kneeling before his disciples to wash their feet, is described as a slave who will be sold "as a slave" that night by Judas. Vieira, by underscoring the image of the suffering servant, sees the relationship of God and humanity in terms of service and loving condescension without expectation of reciprocity. Love of God transcends the reasonable. Christ's new commandment of love runs counter to human love because it obliges that each of us love everyone, including those who persecute us, who betray us, in short, even our enemies. In human love, jealousy includes hatred, implying possessiveness and exclusion: "When they love, it is on the condition that they don't love others and that others don't love them."[28] Divine love obliges all to love all.

Whereas Vieira maintains a distinction between Christ's love and our human love, Sor Juana emphasizes the equality of partners and remains consistently within the framework of erotic love in her description of divine love. God's jealousy is that of a lover who not only wants to be loved, but wants it known that he is loved (OC 4:427–28). "If I cease being jealous it is a sign that I have ceased loving you" (OC 4:427.620–21). Christ's command to the disciples to mutual service cannot be interpreted as a substitute for loving God, or Christ. The symbolic gesture of the foot washing indicates that the most effective way of *expressing* love of God is through love of neighbor (OC 4:425.519–27). As lover, Christ does not want to be "unrequited." Since reciprocal love can only be given in freedom, God has given human beings freedom so that they can enter into a deeper relationship with God. The nun's use of the metaphor of passionate lovers to elaborate the ideal relationship between God and humans, highlighting similarity/equality and emotion (jealousy), exists in tension with her accents on the logical and metaphysical/ontological in other phases of her argument with Vieira.

Finally, both writers use models which run counter to the prevailing ecclesiastical and political power structure. Vieira through inversion of the expected master/slave, ruler/subject relationship; Sor Juana in her emphasis on equality and reciprocal exchange. Yet the different choice of metaphors points to a crucial difference between the Mexican nun and the Brazilian priest: their respective gender. The model Vieira has chosen reflects his own position of power and influence, as well as that of his audience—the royal court. Only someone in a position of superiority can agree to "condescend," to become a slave voluntarily out of love, and does not need to seek corresponding love in order to exist (Vieira's model of Christ's love). Sor Juana, who speaks from a social position of inequality, aspires to equality, and her choice of metaphor for the divine/human relationship as that of lovers reflects this aspiration. Since her power was dependent on another's, she was more likely to conceive of correspondence in love as a necessary component of the greatest demonstration of Christ's love. As a woman, having no pulpit from which to preach, Sor Juana must "enter into correspondence" in order to be heard at all. Even the literary form in which she constitutes this, her one expressly theological work, takes shape in a that genre of correspondence: the letter.

7

The Nun and the Bishop: Drama of Power

Letters which engender pride, are displeasing to God in woman.
> Manuel Fernández de Santa Cruz,
> bishop of Puebla to Sor Juana
> (OC 4:695)

S OR JUANA'S FAR-RANGING literary skills and talent for conversation must have made her a fascinating correspondent. Her first biographer, the Spanish Jesuit, P. Calleja, in his introductory essay to *Fame and Posthumous Works*, writes of their twenty year transatlantic friendship. Unfortunately, no one has as yet found a trace of this correspondence, nor of her correspondence with her friend, the countess of Paredes. However, three letters of a different type, appearing between November 1690 and March 1691, do provide material for the discussion of the crisis at the end of the nun's life. The first is *Athenagoric Letter* discussed in the last chapter. The second is the letter of the bishop of Puebla alias Sor Philotea de la Cruz to Sor Juana which prefaced the edition of *Athenagoric Letter* which he published. The third is Sor Juana's *Response to Sor Philotea de la Cruz*, written several months after the publication of the *Letter*. This particular "exchange" of letters reflects the "ambiguous place between secrecy and publicity" which the letter as a genre occupied.[1] Seventeenth-century letter writers understood that their letters would be read by more than just the addressee, even if they were not published. Copies were kept of letters sent, in the knowledge that they would be circulated and "that sooner or later their opinions" would be "the property of all who read."[2] It was a form cultivated for public consumption beginning with classical Hellenism, when the apostle Paul adopted it. In the Renaissance, letter writing manuals were produced, the most famous being that of Erasmus.[3] In the seventeenth century, Cicero was considered the model writer of letters of news, of society gossip, and of moral deliberations.[4] Sor Juana would have been familiar with his letters from her study of the Latin classics. She knew the famous letters of antiquity, which included those of the patron saint of her order St. Jerome. Closer to her own period were examples of letters used as tools of polemics (Pascal's *Lettres Provincales*, 1656). Letters could also function as an informal frame for pedagogy and spiritual direction, as many collections of letters of churchmen to pious women attest. The most famous seventeenth-century example is the correspondence of Francis de Sales with Louise de Chastel, Mme de Charmoisey, which became the classic *Introduction to a Devout Life* (1609). Two of the powerful churchmen in Sor Juana's life—the Bishop of Puebla, Manuel Fernández de Santa Cruz, and her spiritual director, the Jesuit Núñez de Miranda—had such collections of their letters published. It is against this background that we must consider the unfolding drama of life and letters which began with the publication of the *Athenagoric Letter*. Today it is generally accepted that the addressee of both the *Letter* and the *Response* was the bishop of Puebla, Manuel Fernández de Santa Cruz, a known friend of Sor Juana, who frequented the convent parlor of the Hieronimites.[5] Don Manuel was nominated bishop of Puebla, the second largest episcopal seat after Mexico City, in 1676 at the age of thirty-nine, and remained there until his death in 1699. Author of three volumes of theology that tried to reconcile apparent contradictions in the Bible, he also kept up an extensive correspondence with many nuns. Some thirty-six of his letters, including Sor Philotea's, were published by his biographer, Miguel de Torres, a nephew of Sor Juana.[6]

Because her outstanding intellectual abilities could not be ignored, and because they conflicted with the view of women as intellectually inferior to men, Sor Juana had become adept at rhetorical tactics to subvert common perceptions. Previous chapters have demonstrated various ways she sought to destabilize discourse using devices such as parody, allegory, mimicry of accepted modes of women's behavior, and the "language games" of her time.[7] One of these strategies was manipulation of voice. Sometimes she speaks through the characters of her plays, sometimes through indigenous voices in her liturgical hymns, sometimes developing that of asexual reason, sometimes the voice of a man, sometimes her own woman's voice.[8]

Sor Juana's awareness of the transgressive nature of this particular act of writing is already evident in the opening and closing sections of the *Letter*. She employs a variety of rhetorical strategies to diminish what she anticipates as offensive in her sortie onto theological terrain. Three strategies in particular are intended to protect and affirm her identity as feminine author. She seeks the benevolence of her male interlocutor by ostensibly conforming to the prevailing view of women as subject to men (obedience). She claims to be less capable (humility topics) than men.[9] She engages in "contradictory speech acts," simultaneously denying and affirming her authorial voice.[10]

Opening with a stock rhetorical convention of writers of her time, especially religious, the nun, as in the case of *Alegorical Neptune*, claims to be writing "under obedience."[11] When she writes, therefore, it is not her will which is responsible for the resulting product, but that of the *señor* she addresses. She stresses that she is following her custom of obeying the addressee in the most difficult matters: In this case the elevated topic, but also, more importantly, the request to criticize, which goes "against her deepest inclinations."

In a second step, Sor Juana emphasizes that even in its purpose and technique her voice is derivative, this time of the intent and method of the other masculine voice in the conversation, Vieira, who claims to have successfully disproved Augustine, Thomas Aquinas, and John Chrysostom concerning the proofs of Christ's love. The nun professes to be emboldened by the example of this "modern Cicero," who dares challenge the three *canonized* writers, in order to justify her own critique. She further emphasizes the imitative aspect of her undertaking by "candidly" adopting Vieira's method: to present the views of the saints, and then her own.

A third authoritative support for her undertaking to write moves from the human to the divine. She will "defend her position with the arguments of the three Holy Fathers" (Augustine, Aquinas, John Chrysostom), whom she also describes as "giants" and "more than human." In a final step, the nun portrays herself as speaking as God's instrument. Just as God elects those whom the world perceives as poor and ignorant to confound the wise, so she, an ignorant woman, is God's means of punishing the presumptuous Vieira, "a male (*varón*) illustrious in all respects" (OC 4:435). At the same time, the classical reference she uses as an embellishment underscores her consciousness of the irony of the device: She is like a pygmy beside the herculean Vieira. "What is a poor woman to do?" Although everyone knows, she reminds her readers that it was a woman who took the club from the hands of Hercules, "one of the three impossible tasks venerated by Antiquity"[12] (OC 4:434.911–16). Other details of this particular myth, replete with power and gender reversals which Sor Juana omits, would have been known to her contemporaries. As punishment for killing a friend in a fit of rage, Hercules is sent to be the slave of the Lydian queen, Omphale, who forced him to wear women's clothes and spin wool with her maids while she wore his famous lionskin and carried his club.[13]

Sor Juana uses such expressions as "*una pobre mujer*" (a lowly woman) or "*una mujer ignorante*" always in an indirect, ironic manner. Although, in her conclusion, the nun apologizes for the crudeness, brevity, and lack of scholarship of her letter, coming where it does—at the end of a brilliant polished refutation of Vieira—it is once again an ironic salute to a literary convention rather than a judgment of her work. A comparison to Teresa of Ávila's use of this technique is instructive. Alison Weber has shown that in contrast to male writers, Teresa includes "humility topics" in the body of her work, rather than just in the prologue, and offers "two or three topics per page."[14] Weber sees this as a sign of Teresa's precarious position as a woman mystic, which required her to request repeatedly "the benevolent cooperation of her audience and at the same time 'disavow her abilities and favors.'"[15]

The third major rhetorical device, that of "contradictory speech acts," or affirming while denying, is an integral part of the structure of her "denial of her own voice." This is especially evident in the opening and closing of the *Letter*. In the opening sentence, Sor Juana suggests her authorship in the seemingly frivolous, and therefore non-threatening, context of a parlor "conversation." By describing how the ideas she is about to put to paper came "suddenly, spontaneously to her," she is able to disavow any premeditated intent to criticize Vieira. Though she begins by saying that she wants to defend the arguments of "the three Holy Fathers," lest this seem too forward she immediately corrects herself: her intention is to "defend her position with the arguments of the three Holy Fathers." She underscores the distinction just made by a parenthetical, "Now I think I have expressed myself properly" (OC 4:413.70). Nonetheless, by leaving her initial misformulation in the text rather than erasing it, she suggests that it is not inconceivable that she "defend the Fathers" with her own voice, and that her restatement is one of convenience rather than conviction.

At the closing of her critique of Vieira, Sor Juana makes the conventional cautionary disclaimer of heretical opinion, but with extraordinary vehemence. She writes: "I detest and declare nullified and *not spoken* anything which deviates from the common opinion of our Holy Mother Church and that of the Holy Fathers"[16] (OC 4:435.945–48). The double dynamic of her denial of her own voice is once again revealed. Even as she is disavowing her own authorial voice, she is the one voicing the denial. Whereas she appears here to be the mouthpiece of Holy Mother Church, she is claiming jurisdiction over her own words by declaring, "as not spoken" (*por no dicho*) or as "erased", anything which might be regarded as heretical. By so doing, she is claiming a right of interpretation of her own statements. In the instant she declares nullified something she has written, she has assumed her own authority and authorship.

CRITIQUE

IN THE PROCESS of constructing a space for her speech through the assumption of derivative voice, Sor Juana has managed to enter the world of male discourse, through which, even as an "echo" thereof, she assumes the power of critique. She is careful to say she is a "reluctant critic" in general, because her disposition (*genio*) finds confrontation repugnant. She finds it particularly difficult in Vieira's case because, in addition to her admiration of his rhetorical brilliance, he has earned her special admiration for a number of reasons: by his devotion to his faith, by his talent for theology, and because of a secret sympathy which she harbors for his country, Portugal.[17] His claim, however, to exceed the wisdom of Augustine, Aquinas, and John Chrysostom by irrefutable arguments has moved her to write. She cites Vieira directly here and repeats: "These are his exact words, this is his proposal, and this is what has motivated my response" (OC 4:414.85–86). In so doing Sor Juana configures herself as the modest woman, Vieira as the arrogant (male) scholar, and she calls on the bishop to use his authority to cover "the errors of her obedience to his command" which to other eyes would appear due to disproportionate pride, even more so from "one of a sex so discredited in matter of letters as everyone agrees" (OC 4:412.27–28).

In addition to the stereotype of the presumptuous female scholar, Sor Juana rebuts the cliché of woman as excessively emotional. She exhorts the addressee to see "how purified of all passion her reasoning will be" (OC 4:412.29–30). Not that she does not experience passion or emotion. Her positive "reasons" for not criticizing the Jesuit are in the affective order: she shares his love for his religion, admires his rhetorical skill, has an affinity for his nation. Her negative grounds are also those of affect: fear of being misunderstood, of being considered a heretic. All these "reasons" she argues might suffice to silence her, but they are not enough to vanquish human understanding, "a free power which assents or dissents necessarily to that which it judges to be or not to be true" (OC 4:413.42–43).

Octavio Paz has pointed out how often Sor Juana speaks of the soul as "having no sex"[18] which he considers evidence of her rejection of feminine voice in favor of the universally "human" power of intellect. Yet, in *Athenagoric Letter*, she frames her arguments with language of desire and response, engendering and birth. So the opening sentence speaks of the birth of desire, and of pleasure as response and motivation. And she repeats in her second paragraph: "We spoke of this and it pleased you (as I have said) to see this written" (OC 4:412.17). At her closing of the *Letter* she laments that, just as "the bitch who in great haste gives birth to her blind pups," she has hastily brought her offspring, the text, to term. With hesitation, she sends her argument forth "in embryo, . . . as the she-bear gives birth to her formless cubs" (OC 4:434.904). Though considering a book as one's child was a common literary topos—which Cervantes satirized in his prologue to *Don Quixote*[19]— and the she-bear with her cub was a common emblem of the artistic process in the Renaissance,[20] the nun twice casts herself in the role of an animal parent rather than a human one, further accentuating her "unworthiness" as part of what Oliver has shown to be her elaborate strategies of (self)irony.[21]

SOR PHILOTEA'S VEILED PREFACE

SOR JUANA'S CAUTIONARY strategies in the *Letter* were well founded, if not successful, in warding off criticism. Constance Montross points out: "The Bishop's reply to Sor Juana indicates that her obsession with explaining her motives and position, and her fears of being misunderstood (in the *Letter*) are justified."[22] Recognizing the rhetorical game Sor Juana was playing, the bishop, through "Sor Philotea's" letter, seeks to rob her of the voice which, with elaborate caution, she sought to establish in the opening and closing of the *Letter*.

His most obvious assertion of power is his publication of her work against her express request, thereby making it clear that the destiny of the *Letter* is not in her hands, but in those of another. He also changed the name of her treatise from her own "*Critique of a Sermon (Crisis de un sermon)*, the name given it on its publication in Seville in 1692, to the complimentary "Letter Worthy of Athena" (*Athenagoric Letter*). In so doing, he has taken her out of the "inappropriate" public sphere of a critic of sermons and put her back in the, at least ostensibly, private sphere of letterwriting. Even the comparison to the goddess of wisdom has taken the edge off the challenge to male authority. Athena, the goddess of unnatural origin, was born not of woman, but sprung from the head of Zeus.

Perhaps the bishop's most ingenious strategy is the assumption of a female pseudonym. Many interpreters see it as a gesture of condescension, designed by its presumption of familiarity and equality, to take the edge off what is a criticism of her life and work.[23] More nuanced, Jean Franco remarks that though the bishop probably considered "he was doing Sor Juana a favor by abandoning the authority of his position and reprimanding her as a friend and equal," he was obviously aware that the effect of the "transvestite disguise," similar to that of rebaptizing her work, was to reinforce her exclusion from the circle of male discourse.[24] Josefina Ludmer considers this device instrumental in framing the space from which Sor Juana, in her *Response*, forges the chain of veiled knowledge and feigned ignorance, of constructed silence and tangled speech which constitute the strategies of the weak.[25] In effect, it signals that Sor Juana's only appropriate partner in (public) theological discourse is a woman, and it forces the nun to deal with what is in essence a fictional character, a masked identity, to participate in a fictional conversation if she were to respond. Furthermore, since the blurring of the lines between staged drama and the drama of life are favorite baroque typoi, it is possible that is part of the bishop's game.[26] Even the names of the real and the fictional "characters" echo each other: Mañuel Fernández de Santa Cruz becomes Sor Philotea de la Cruz in order to publicly engage in discussion with Sor Juana Inés de la Cruz.

The particular name which the bishop chooses—"Philotea" (literally "lover of God")—has historical/biographical connotations as well as textual implications. Its literal meaning serves to strengthen the invitation to Sor Juana to leave secular letters for holy pursuits, a function emphasized by the worldly or heathen name which the bishop has attached to the nun, Athena. Ludmer sets up a similar contrast, but compares Philotea (lover of God) with an implied Sor Philosophia (Sor Juana) whose athenagoric letter means to refer to the wisdom of Athenian philosophers rather than to the wisdom of the goddess Athena.[27] To contemporaries, it would recall the *Introduction to the Devout Life* by Francis de Sales (1567–1622), the esteemed French bishop and spiritual writer who gave the name *Philothée* to his "spiritual daughter" Louise de Chastel when he published his letters to her. "I address my discourse to Philothea, because, from a desire to reduce what I had at first written for one only, to the general advantage of many souls, I make use of a name applicable to all who aspire to devotion. For Philothea signifies a soul loving, or in love with God."[28] Fernández de Santa Cruz, also a known admirer of Francis de Sales, may have sought a benevolent comparison through his use of the same name, a connection suggested in the prefaces for the last volume of Sor Juana's works, *Fame and Posthumous Works*.[29] A second connection, closer to Mexico, has been suggested by Dorothy Schons: Fernández de Santa Cruz was saluting his predecessor as bishop of Puebla, Juan de Palafox y Mendoza. Palafox, in imitation of Francis de Sales, had written *Pilgrimage of Filotea to the Holy Temple and Hill of the Cross* which enjoyed great popularity.[30] The link to Francis de Sales also has the intriguing consequence of Sor Juana's being "taught" by the, albeit in this case fictional, "spiritual daughter" (Filotea) of a famous, pious bishop, the real Fernández de Santa Cruz. As Angelo Morino has remarked, the pseudonym was intended to be transparent not only to the nun, but to all the aristocrats and intellectuals of New Spain.[31]

The bishop's praise of Sor Juana is conditional and ambiguous, beginning with the first paragraph which is a panegyric of Vieira and his teacher César Meneses, acclaimed by the most learned of towering intellects. This contrasts with the subdued tones and negative turns of phrase in which the bishop describes the nun's refutation of Vieira: "Those who read your apologia could not deny that your pen was cut finer than theirs." And: "They might boast of seeing themselves opposed by a woman who is an honor to her sex" (OC 4:694). In fact, the bishop is beginning what is a two pronged sally to defend the Jesuit from Sor Juana's accusation of arrogance and to accuse her of the same. In his first paragraph he counters Sor Juana's basic assertion that the proud man (*varón*) Vieira would be humbled by being refuted by a woman who "dared to respond" (OC 4:435.931–33): first, by not responding to her "as a male"; second, by writing that both the Jesuit and his illustrious teacher Meneses would be proud (*gloriarse*) to find themselves refuted "by a woman who is the honor of her sex." He, thereby, suggests that they are not too proud to accept reasoned refutation even from a woman.

The second paragraph praises Sor Juana's clarity of expression, but even this is qualified by being associated with worldly wisdom. Christ's supreme wisdom was not clear, but veiled in parables which were not admired by "the world." Even the clarity of her writing, however, is not her own, but a gift of God's. "Clarity is not acquired with work and diligence, rather it is a gift infused in the soul" (OC 4:694). By moving the nun's talents into the realm of the charismatic, i.e., God given, the bishop is, in fact, taking control of the possibility that more women might, through learning, be able to do what she does.

Throughout his letter, Santa Cruz stresses his own liberality and good will toward Sor Juana by comparing his attitude with that of other less generous critics.

> I, at least, have admired the liveliness of your ideas. . . .
> My judgement is not such a severe censor that it would
> criticize your writing of verses . . . I do not approve of
> the vulgarity of those who deny women learning . . . I do
> not claim that . . . you modify your genius by renounc-
> ing books . . . I do not censure the reading of such
> (pagan) authors.[32]

As Montross has noticed, this "line of argument allows him to hint at further actions should Sor Juana not obey him now."[33]

A further result of the bishop's situating himself as a moderate is to increase the impact of his *many expressly* negative comments which are cited here together:

> I fear that you are arrears in your payment of what you owe to God, as few creatures have received as many natural gifts as you. . . . Though you have done well enough up to this point, may you do better in the future. . . . I would wish that you imitate . . . [Saint Teresa] not only in choice of meter, but also in choice of subject. . . . I wish you would sometimes read the book of Jesus Christ. . . . You have wasted much time in the study of philosophy and poetry. It is about time that you perfect your use of time and improve your choice of books. . . . It is a pity that your great understanding should become confused by the despicable things of the earth and not desire to penetrate heaven. As it is already bent down to the ground, take care that it does not descend to those things of Hell. . . . Apply your understanding to the Mount of Calvary where you will see the demonstrations of love of the Redeemer and the ingratitude of the redeemed. There you will find a great field for pondering the excesses of divine love and space to form apologias, not without tears, against an ingratitude which reaches the heights. O how useful if on other occasions the rich galleon of your genius would embark on the high sea of divine perfections. . . . I am very certain and sure that if you, with the lively discourse of your mind, would form and paint a picture of the divine perfections . . . would see at the same time your soul enlightened and your will aflame and sweetly wounded with the love of its God, so that the Lord who has showered so abundantly positive benefits on you in the natural order, will not be obligated to concede you only negative benefits in the eternal order.[34]

Fernández de Santa Cruz's motivations for writing his preface, as well as his publishing Sor Juana's work, remain as ambiguous as the nun's situation itself. He is obviously strongly suggesting a conversion on her part: She should sometimes read the book of Jesus Christ, imitate Saint Teresa, etc.[35] Many questions remain unanswered however, if we accept this simple explanation. Would the bishop need to engage in the elaborate subterfuge of writing under a pseudonym? Since they were friends, why write to her at all? Why would he finance the publication of the *Letter* "into the world" while at the same time criticizing her involvement in "the world?" Why did he publish her theological treatise claiming to belong to the tradition of Saint Jerome, who encouraged that women study if not teach, if he did not want to encourage her to write more theology?

Critics have given numerous reasons for the bishop's publication of the letter and his assumption of female identity. Patricio Lizama sees the bishop's entire form as a classical call to conversion as understood in the Christian tradition.[36] Paz views it as part of a scheme, in alliance with Sor Juana, to criticize and embarrass the misogynist archbishop of Mexico City, Aguiar y Seijas, a supporter and admirer of Vieira and the Jesuits[37] who would have found criticism especially galling coming from a woman. The feminine pseudonym would have been Santa Cruz's means of protecting himself as publisher from Aguiar y Seijas.

Though Paz insists that Sor Juana was more than the instrument of Fernández de Santa Cruz, he sees an essential dependency.

> She would never have written that text without the support of the Bishop of Puebla: the Letter was addressed to him; he wrote the ecclesiastical imprimatur that allowed it to be published; he wrote the prologue; and he bore the costs of publication. Sor Juana could not have foreseen the consequences of her act. She felt secure in the protection of powerful patrons in Madrid and Mexico.[38]

My view is that the publication of the *Letter* and Santa Cruz's preface is less conspiratorial than Paz would suggest, but less kindly than others imply.[39] In their historical studies, Alatorre and Bénassy emphasize the support, even in ecclesiastical circles, that Sor Juana enjoyed. Bénassy is especially intent on arguing that Agiar y Seijas, Núñez de Miranda, and even Fernández de Santa Cruz had only the welfare of Sor Juana's soul in mind. The strength of these interpretations is their close examination of historical documents, of the lives of the churchmen in question, and of contemporary responses to Sor Juana. However, they fail to take into account "the implicit prohibitions" on writing operative in any society, that are at least doubled when the author was a woman living in an age and a country in which the Inquisition was very much alive. Here Paz's caution is to be observed: "Her work tells us something, but to understand that something we must realize that it is utterance surrounded by silence: the silence of the *things that cannot be said.*"[40]

The bishop himself gives two reason for his publishing: that Sor Juana better "see herself" through the printed version, and that she become filled with greater recognition of the gifts God has given her. In essence, he intends the printed form of the *Letter* framed by his prologue, to serve as a mirror which will enable the nun to see herself as he sees her, recognize her faults and begin a conversion to a better life. The language he uses to formulate his "desire" is symptomatic of the "game" level of his letter, and also a sign that the subversive subtext of the *Letter* has not escaped him. "*Para que V. md. se vea en este papel de mejor letra*" (OC 4:694) is the beginning of a word game constructed around multiple meanings of the words *letra* and *papel.* In the context of publishing the *Letter, papel* can be considered paper and *letra* the print on the page. Thus Trueblood's translation: "So that you may read yourself in clearer lettering in that document." However, *papel* in its meaning of "role" is also implied, and reference to *mejor letra* (better letter) takes on a second meaning in the context of another game played around *señor/a* two paragraphs later.

It is at this point in his text that Santa Cruz distances himself from the "vulgar" opinion which would limit "the use of letters in women" and agrees with St. Jerome's praise of studious women. Furthermore he sides with a "liberal" interpretation of St. Paul which allowed women to study, but forbade them from teaching to prevent the risk of pride "in our sex, which is always predisposed to vanity" (OC 4:695). Scripture is clear on the position of women as subordinate to men. "Divine Wisdom took a letter" from Sarai, to make it Sara, but added one to Abram (Abraham), (Gn 17:5, 15), not because, as many maintain, that the man (*varón* or male) should *tener más letras* (have more learning), but because it was not fitting that his wife have a name which as Sarai meant *Señora mía,* implying "fear and domination in one who was a subordinate (*subdita*)" (OC 4:695). The bishop concludes by returning to St. Paul: "Letters engendering pride, God does not want in women," but St. Paul does not object as long as their learning does not disturb their condition or state of obedience (*estado de obediente*). Though he insists that "everyone knows" that Sor Juana's learning and knowledge have served to perfect her obedience, even emphasizing that she offers not only her will (as do other religious), but also her intellect "on the altars of religion," but given the tenor of the remainder of his text, these remarks must be seen as a wish or an ironic statement. The main thrust of his remarks is again that Sor Juana, not Vieira, is arrogant, with an arrogance not only unbecoming to a woman, but forbidden by God because it threatens her divinely ordained subordinate role.

Several paragraphs later, servant/master metaphors emerge as Santa Cruz reproaches the nun for preferring secular to sacred study. "Humanistic studies are slaves and should be used to advantage by (for) divine studies. They should be reprimanded, however, when they turn human understanding from Divine wisdom, making themselves *señoras* when they are meant to be servants" (OC 4:696). In a sly aside, the bishop of Puebla de los *Angeles* remarks that even St. Jerome (the founder of Sor Juana's order) was scourged by angels for reading Cicero with too much avidity to the neglect of scripture.

The bishop's second principal reproach is Sor Juana's lack of gratitude. The many gifts she has received from God have led her to a major error in thinking: her position on "negative benefits" as the greatest *fineza* of divine love. Santa Cruz would see all grace as "positive" in nature, preparing the soul for future good works, disposing it for more gratitude, so that it becomes ever more open to the torrents of divine liberality (OC 4:696). If she were more appropriately conscious of the gifts God has given her, she would turn from worldly things to heavenly.

In his closing, Santa Cruz speaks of his long association with her in the many years since their first meeting, during which he has lived "enamored of her soul." He prays God to make her holy and signs off with the obviously ambiguous, "your *afecta* servant." At the literal level, *afecta* signifies affectionate, at the game level of the text, "pretended."

MASKING AND UNMASKING

LITTLE IS KNOWN about what happened in the months between the publication of the *Letter* in December 1690 and the completion of Sor Juana's *Response to Sor Filotea de la Cruz*, March 1, 1691. The only written record is a pamphlet, the text of a sermon preached in March of 1691 in Sor Juana's own convent. A Valencian priest,

Francisco-Javier Palavicino, took issue with *both* Vieira and Sor Juana on the greatest demonstration of Christ's love.[41] However the opening passages of the sermon praise both the nun and the Jesuit: Sor Juana is "the most select talent . . . Minerva of America, great talent limited only by the impediment of being a woman . . . whose works have received general acclamation and praise . . . of the greatest intellects of Europe."[42] Bénassy-Berling considers Palavicino's sermon as an example of nascent Criollo pride, conquering the antifeminism "of at least a segment of the clergy," as well as proof that it was possible in the Archdiocese of Mexico, even as governed by the misogynist Aguiar y Seijas, that a priest could publish praise of Sor Juana.[43] This incident, for Bénassy, is part of her case against a *general ecclesiastical* hostility toward Sor Juana. Paz interprets the preaching of this sermon as part of a prudent policy of the Hieronimite nuns who wanted to demonstrate their impartiality by inviting someone to take a position different from Sor Juana's on the demonstration of Christ's love.[44] It is one piece of evidence in his theory which sees her composition of the *Letter* as part of a plan to embarrass Aguiar y Seijas, a supporter and admirer of Vieira, through the critique of a woman. For Paz it is symptomatic again of the complexity of clerical relations in seventeenth-century Hispanic society, in which rival theologies masked personal and political antagonistisms.[45]

As we have seen in connection with Sor Juana's poetry and drama, as well as in her correspondence with Bishop Santa Cruz, there is a convergence between the Baroque devices of costuming, role playing, and literary word games and Sor Juana's transgressive message. Recent interpretations of the *Response* explore many of them: the functioning of multi-leveled irony;[46] the use of quotations from the Bible and Christian and pagan antiquity to deliver double messages;[47] application of principles of classical rhetoric;[48] and deployment of strategies of feminine authorship.[49]

Such studies, as well as comparison with the directness and self-assertion of the earlier private letter of Monterrey, make it impossible to continue to accept interpretations such as those of Sor Juana's twentieth-century editor Salceda that ignore any hint of subtext or complication of context. I quote him here by way of contrast:

> His excellency Fernández de Santa Cruz advises her to pursue better occupations, but he neither reproves, persecutes or harassses her. She remains free as before, but she has listened to a wise and affectionate voice of common sense.

> This is the manner in which she receives it, understands it, and esteems it as she describes the letter as "most learned, most discreet, most holy, and most loving" and responds with a thousand tokens of profound gratitude and without one single word of resentment or displeasure in the justly celebrated *Response to Sor Philotea de la Cruz.*[50]

Sor Juana's skill at manipulating irony is at work in the opening of the *Response* where she frames her introduction as an apology for her tardy response to a letter which did not anticipate a response. She begins by explaining her period of "silence," when in reality, silence was the expected response. To respond to the letter, she would have had to do two "impossible" things. The first was to write a response worthy of Philotea's "most learned, most discreet, most holy, and most loving letter." She is silent, not out of the virtue of humility, as was Thomas Aquinas before his teacher Albertus Magnus, but because she "*in reality*" did not know anything to say worthy of her/him (OC 4:440.13). The reality in this case is, of course, obscured because of the fictional character of the addressee.

The second "impossibility" was being incapable of thanking him/her for the "most minimal part" of what she owed him for the "unhoped for and excessive favor . . . the grace without measure going beyond the most ambitious hope, the most fantastic of desires, beyond that which, as a reasoning being, might be contained in her thought" of printing her "scribblings" (OC 4:440.12–18). The irony beyond the hyperbole is contained in the contradiction between these sentiments and Sor Juana's express prohibition of the publication, implying *fear* that it might be published.[51]

Philotea is like God, who corrects most people by punishment, but "wants to reduce me through benefits" (OC 4:441.50–51), a theme she had developed in the *Letter*. Put another way, God, by not granting her "negative benefits" (i.e., the non-publication of her work), is punishing her by burdening her with a debt which she cannot possibly repay: sufficient gratitude to Sor Philotea.

SOR JUANA UNMASKS THE BISHOP

IN ORDER TO answer Philotea's letter "in reality" Sor Juana undertakes to reveal her/his identity. In 1682 in her earlier letter to the Jesuit Núñez de Miranda, Sor Juana constructed the image of her interlocutor, as one critic maintains, by proceeding to advance, then retreat, conceding, yet relativizing the principle of authority which Núñez represents. This is even more so the case in the *Response*.[52] Ostensibly, her friend Santa Cruz has proven himself able to "play games" by donning the persona of a woman in order to answer Sor Juana, as I indicated in the preceding section. Though no one in Mexico City would have been deceived by his pen name, but because a simple nun could not grant permission to publish, Sor Juana was not at liberty to address Santa Cruz as the real author. Instead, with a degree of playfulness that belies the seriousness of the game in which she is engaged, she begins a textual construction that is designed "to disclose the real character behind the mask to be the powerful bishop, not the nun".[53]

This gender masquerade of bishop and nun was not as surprising in seventeenth-century Mexico, where pageantry was still a part of everyday life, as it might appear to us today. One of the most common forms was the *máscara*, a parade in which all classes participated, disguised as allegorical figures, important persons, stock folk characters, as well as famous characters from romances (including Don Quixote). Participants could be found roaming the streets by day or night.[54] Cross-dressing for special occasions was also a more commonly accepted practice than today. Leonard records an entire *máscara* in which men dressed as women, women as men. In drama, crossdressing served to complicate the process of self-revelation of character and resolution of plot, and to set an ironic frame around contemporary understanding of the role of the sexes. Though women dressing as men was common, Sor Juana's drama, *The Trials of a Noble House*, contains a more unusual case of a man dressing as a woman. Don Sanchez's servant, the farcical Castaño, dresses in the clothes of the heroine Leonor as a courier of her secret suitor. In a comic fashion he examines each piece of clothing and comments on its function to the audience as he puts it on (OC 4:135–39).[55]

In the *Response*, Sor Juana proceeds to take off the mask of powerlessness which Sor Philotea had assumed in her transvestite identity. She begins with the greeting: "Very illustrious lady, my lady" instead of the simpler "*Muy Señor mío*" of the *Letter* or the "*Señora mía*" of Sor Philotea's letter to her. A further device is to contrast high praise of the addressee to her own meager powers. Though this was a stock convention in the epistolary tradition, for Sor Juana the *issue* was her humility and lack of gratitude to God for his bestowal of gifts on her. She does this in a variety of ways.[56] One such strategy is to highlight the actual power relationship between herself and the Bishop through a series of images and comparisons comprising the bulk of the two hundred fifteen line opening. In each case, Sor Philotea is identified as the authority, Sor Juana as the subject. The first is the relationship of teacher to student. This is already an ironic comment on Santa Cruz's textual disguise in which he refers to himself as a "fond student" (*estudiosa aficionada*) of Sor Juana on the cover of the first edition. First, as part of her apology for her delayed response to Philotea, she uses the example of two giants of the medieval schools, Thomas Aquinas and his teacher Albertus Magnus.[57] By identifying Sor Philotea as Albertus Magnus and herself as Thomas Aquinas, she also implies she might supersede her "teacher," Sor Philotea (OC 4:413.42).

Sor Juana persists in reinforcing the picture of "superiority" of the bishop through a series of biblical comparisons. In general, as we have seen, the use of classical and biblical references, in Latin or in the vernacular, always has a peculiar place in Sor Juana's writings, and many times functions as a keys to different levels of meaning or alternative readings of the text. Sor Juana's first example is the scene popularly known as the Visitation (Lk 1:39–56), and functions to set up Sor Juana as the lowly Elizabeth, Philotea/Santa Cruz as the loftier Mary. Like Elizabeth, who Sor Juana describes as "happily sterile", to become miraculously fertile in her old age, so Sor Juana, as a nun "sterile" by definition of her celibacy, is able to become "miraculously fertile" as a woman writer. Like Mary, whom Sor Juana names only as "Mother of the Word", Fernández de Santa Cruz can be read as "mother/father" of the word(s) Sor Juana has written in three respects: as addressee of the *Letter* by suggesting she write it; as bishop/ Philotea, by publishing it; and by engendering her subsequent *Response* through his public criticism in Philotea's letter.

A subsidiary technique, operating within the Mary/Elizabeth parallel, is Sor Juana's use of Latin quotations to allow her to "say the words" which would otherwise remain unspoken.[58] In this case, she compares her own speechlessness when receiving the published *Letter* to Elizabeth's initial response to Mary's visit: "understanding is darkened and her speech suspended." Elizabeth's question "Why to me?" (*Et unde hoc mihi?*) operates as a question to the bishop:

What has she done to deserve the publication of her critique of Vieira's sermon?[59] Similarly, in her first Old Testament example (1 Sm 9:21), the true power relationship of nun and bishop is again highlighted. In this case, Saul's (Sor Juana's) protestation of his/her unworthiness, as least important member of the smallest tribe of Israel, when Samuel (the bishop) comes to anoint him king, also allows her to repeat her cry of indignation. Again, in Spanish and in Latin: "Why say this to me? Why me? (*Et unde hoc mihi?*) Whereas the two preceding examples present Sor Juana's stunned surprise at the "favor" granted, the two succeeding ones serve to "explain" her movement from silence into speech (OC 4:442–43. 100–116). In the first, the nun compares herself to Moses, "a stutterer," who at first needed Aaron as his voice when speaking to Pharaoh; later, because of God's many favors (the bishop's gracious condescension), she dares ask him to do something impossible: "*Ostende mihi faciem tuam*" (Show me your face); "Thus, so do I," interjects Sor Juana at this point. The Latin text which fuses Ex 33:18 (Show me your glory) and Ex 33:20 (My face you cannot see, for no mortal may see me and live) serves again as a direct challenge to Santa Cruz to "take off his mask."

Another biblical couple is taken from the Book of Esther. The Jewish concubine Esther enters the Assyrian king's presence unannounced, a crime punishable by death, in order to intercede for her people. Upon seeing her, the king extends his scepter to spare her, and she kisses it. Sor Juana's description of Philotea as "another Ahasuerus giving me the tip of the golden scepter of your affection to kiss as a sign of conceding me the benevolent license to speak" is rich in associations with the bishop Sor Juana is addressing (OC 4:442. 115–16). First and most obviously, in the seventeenth-century Mexican church, the bishop was the official who licensed the publication of books. Like Ahasuerus, Santa Cruz gives her "license to speak. Another dimension of Ahasuerus's character is that he is the despotic ruler of a "foreign," i.e., non-Jewish, power. In this respect, the Persian king corresponds to Santa Cruz on two levels: as a Spaniard in Mexico and as a male ruler in a world of women, the convents, where a bishop was actually the ultimate authority. Sor Juana, of course, is Esther, the fearful, yet courageous woman interceding on behalf of her people, women, and, if the text is read at another level as an example of nascent criollo nationalism, also for Mexicans. Furthermore, the image of kissing the scepter resonates both with the symbolism of the bishop's staff and of the custom of kissing his ring, and contrasts to the bishop's closing reference of kissing Sor Juana's hand "on first meeting her years ago."

EMOTIONAL RESPONSES

SOR JUANA'S DESCRIPTION of her emotional reaction to receiving the *Letter* also operates on multiple levels. "I broke, (*prorrumpí*) (which is not very easy for me) into tears of confusion" (OC 4:440.28). This emotional breaking has been prefigured on an intellectual level through the example of the Visitation of "the Mother of the Word" (the bishop), which is described as dulling Elizabeth/Sor Juana's understanding and "suspending speech" (*suspendió el discurso*). Elizabeth's first reaction, like Sor Juana's, was not to be grateful, but to break into *prorrumpió* (doubts and questions). On one level, the Elizabeth story would indicate confusion because of thanks due to so great a favor, but Sor Juana's response as it unfolds is more nuanced: "It appeared to me that your favor was no less than a reprimand that God was making to me for the poor way in which I respond to him; and though, with others he corrects by punishing, he wants to reduce me through benefits" (OC 4:441.47–53). Through all her professions of gratitude, Sor Juana maintains her position on "negative benefits" as the greatest *fineza*, the one theological point in the *Letter* to which the bishop objected. By publishing the *Letter* he ends up punishing and humiliating the nun, leaving open the conclusion that the "withholding" of the benefit of publication would have been a greater *fineza*, a greater demonstration of love on his part.

Sor Juana's "tears of confusion" also link the *Response* back to the *Letter* where she theorizes on the nature of tears. Great suffering or distress causes a momentary suspension of faculties (*suspensión de todas las acciónes y movimientos*) after which tears come, releasing the pent up anguish (OC 4:419.284). The paragraph describing Elizabeth's reaction indicates the first response: speech was suspended (*suspendió el discurso*); the description of receiving the *Letter* (I broke into tears) the second. Another point about tears, which Sor Juana makes in the *Letter*, is that, in and of themselves as signs, they are ambivalent. Sometimes they reflect joy, sometimes sorrow. We are left to speculate what emotion was the source of Sor Juana's "tears of confusion." Joy, indignation, rage? Or is her construction of the scene of her reception of the *Letter* a literary device designed to follow to the letter Santa Cruz's charge that she "form an apology, *not without tears*," for her ingratitude which "reached the heights" (OC 4:696)?

Sor Juana Lets Slip Her Mask

Though all through the *Response* she is answering dimensions of Santa Cruz's criticism of her way of life, Sor Juana's defense of her writing the *Letter* breaks out with especial vehemence in lines 1166–98. Here, momentarily dropping her pretense of accepting the mild reproach of an admiring friend, she reveals her actual perception of the preface as the accusation of a crime (*crimen*) (OC 4:468.1165). "If there is a crime in the *Athenagoric Letter*, was it any more than simply to give an account of my opinion, with all the permissions that I owe, to our Holy Mother Church?" (Which, of course, is not a crime.) After enumerating other reasons in support of her innocence in a tone of moral outrage, she "catches herself" and again puts on her official persona, asking: "But, where am I going, *Señora mía*? This is not appropriate here," because as she says, she has been treating Santa Cruz/Philotea as though he were one of her "adversaries" (OC 4:469.1193, 1195), which, of course, he is.

A biblical story involving two women is again a vehicle for disclosure of the two inadmissible emotions: anger and frustration, which have caused Sor Juana's outburst quoted above. Of her literary creation, the *Letter*, she writes:

> If I could have foreseen the fortunate destiny to which it was born when I threw it, like another Moses, to be exposed in the waters of the Nile of silences, where it was found and caressed by a princess like you, I think . . . . I would strangle it with the same hands that gave it birth, for fear the clumsy scribbling of my ignorance should appear before the light of your knowledge (OC 4:471. 1272–79).

Sor Juana, mother of the literary child, *Letter*, is Moses' mother, who places him in the river Nile. Santa Cruz is the Egyptian princess, who rescues Moses/*Letter* from "silence" by its publication. The image is also part of Sor Juana's denial of Sor Philotea's claim to publish the *Letter* in order that Sor Juana have a better appreciation of "the treasures which God has placed in your soul" by seeing her work in print (OC 4:694). On the contrary, its publication, she insists, has made her more than ever aware of its shortcomings, which were due to her lack of time, poor health, necessity of obeying—shortcomings that her critics have discovered, which, Sor Juana implies, were due to practical circumstances, *not to her lack of ability* to write a more perfect treatise.

As she closes the *Response*, she makes clear references to the over-familiarity with which she has engaged while "treating you like a veiled religious, my sister, I may have forgotten the distance from your illustrious person, which I would not have done had I seen you with no veil" (OC 4:474.1419–26). She did not dare "exceed the limits" of Sor Philotea's style, nor "break the margin of your modesty" (OC 4:475.1430–31). Excusing the informal *vos* with which she addresses Philotea (who used the more formal *Vuestra Merced* with her), she puns that she has used *vos* "because, given the reverence I owe you, it would be scant reverence to 'Your Reverence' you," which would have been tantamount to openly lifting the veil. Thus Sor Juana closes her letter with a pun more elegant, though just as obvious, as the bishop's "affectionate servant."

8

Following Jesus: Confession, Conversion, Apologia

*The logician's sentence moves, as does the straight line, by
the shortest route; the rhetorician's moves like the curve,
along the longest one, but both end up at the same point"*
Sor Juana Inés de la Cruz,
Response to Sor Philotea de la Cruz
(OC 4:450.431–34)

B Y NOW IT IS clear that Sor Juana works constantly with subtexts, characterizations, and veiled allusions. These are especially in evidence in the *Response,* which exhibits a formal intricacy due to the complexity of Sor Juana's existential situation as a woman writing about that very issue. Santa Cruz's reaction to her *Letter* demonstrated that she cannot speak as the voice of "pure reason" or logical demonstration, as she had done, in a society which for the most part believed with Aristotle, that *man* is a rational animal, woman not necessarily. As a result, she is presented with a multiple challenge in responding to his letter. She must counter the predominant view of women represented in the letter of Philotea/ Santa Cruz "Learning may be especially dangerous to women, by nature inclined to vanity," defend poetry, and by extension, the arts, as an activity valued by God. She must rebut the prevailing view that withdrawal from the world is the surest way to salvation, and defend her own personal precocious learning and poetic gift. She develops a three-pronged approach in her defense. The first involves a construction of her autobiography, which both mocks and imitates standard autobiography (the subject of this chapter). The second is critique of theological methodology which does not see fit to include and value the testimony of women (Chapter 9). The third is a theory of textual interpretation, which intends to be a key to the interpretation of her own text, the *Response* (Chapter 10).

AUTOBIOGRAPHICAL PROTOTYPES

CRITICS, AGAIN, EMPLOY a range of terms to designate the nature of the autobiographical segments of Sor Juana's *Response*. Franco sees these sections as belonging to a tradition of "confessions," from stock hagiography to Augustine's *Confessions,* and to the self-descriptions of the Hebrew prophets.[1] Lizama would see them as a narrative of failed conversion which accepts the bishop's negative judgment but refuses to accept to change her life.[2] Larisch distinguishes the *Response* from standard autobiography by classifying it as an apology, like Socrates', or Cardinal Newman's, which "places the private in the public domain in order to ward off public calumny and combat the public misunderstanding of a life in the public view."[3] Indeed Sor Juana utilizes all three genres: confession, conversion, and apologia creating "a sort of patchwork that depends on the public aspect"[4] not only of words, but, in this case, "autobiographical" texts of Augustine, Paul, and Socrates.

AUGUSTINE'S CONFESSION

AUGUSTINE AS A theologian was, after Thomas Aquinas, arguably the most influential theologian in the history of Western Christianity. He figures explicitly as one of the three "canonized giants" of the Christian tradition whom Vieira presumes to refute, and Sor Juana defends in *Letter*. In the *Letter of Monterrey,* she uses him as part of her case that scholarship and the religious life can be united. "Are letters an obstacle or do they, rather, lead to salvation? Was not St. Augustine saved . . . ?"[5] His *Confessions* became the model for all future vitae, and, as Sor Juana writes her own, not only does she have him in mind, but her account of her childhood and adolescence can be seen to be a conscious departure from the prototype.[6]

The deviation from the "model life" in this case, puts Sor Juana in virtuous relief against the wandering Augustine who writes: "If I proved idle in learning, I was soundly beaten. . . . It was not, Lord that I lacked mind or memory . . . I disobeyed, not because I had chosen better, but through sheer love of play."[7] The child Juana Inés feared beatings because of her having learned to read. "And I kept silent, believing that they would beat me for having done it without permission" (OC 4:445.231–32). Whereas the future bishop Augustine relates telling many lies to teachers and parents to escape school and run to the theater,[8] the nun recounts lying to be able to learn to read. Continuing chastisement for her interest in learning did not inhibit her: "I found a way to read many different books my grandfather owned, notwithstanding the punishments and reproofs this entailed" (OC 4:446.247–50).[9]

This disjunction persists in texts concerning the rites of passage of young adulthood to sexuality and work. Augustine's academic career was programmed by the ambition of his parents, especially his father, who sent him to the city of Carthage to study to become an orator. The North African's description of his arrival in that university city is memorable (T. S. Eliot includes it in *The Waste Land*), but not because of his academic fervor. "I came to Carthage, where a cauldron of illicit loves leapt and boiled about me."[10] An adult version of the "play" of childhood distracts him from his studies. Whereas in childhood he bent his back to the cane of the schoolmasters, as a youth he writhes in torment under the lashings of love: "I was scourged with the red hot rods of jealousy, with suspicions and fears and tempers and quarrels."[11] Sor Juana's education was self-directed, and it could be argued, even inhibited by her mother. She reports that, when she was seven or eight she heard that there was a university and schools in Mexico City and began to "pester my mother to death," (*matar a mi madre*), to let her dress as a boy to go to study there. Of course, her mother refused. "And it was good that she did" (OC 4: 446.44–45), Sor Juana comments. As a result of her clandestine reading in her grandfather's study, when she did move to Mexico City, people were amazed, "not so much at my talent as at my memory and the amount of information I possessed at an age at which it seemed that I hardly had time to have learned to speak" (OC 4:446.243–47). Part of higher education for both was the learning of a foreign language which, for Sor Juana, was Latin, for

Augustine, Greek. Even in this they differed. Sor Juana voluntarily struggles to learn Latin; Augustine hated learning Greek, and had to be forced to it.[12]

Sor Juana's description of the domination of her natural desires contrasts to Augustine's description of himself, as a slave to all manner of desires of the flesh. Augustine relates how his gluttony caused him to steal food from the pantry and even from his parents' table.[13] Juana Inés stopped eating cheese when she heard it dulled the mind because her "desire to know was greater than the desire to eat, although this is so powerful in children" (OC 4:445. 233–37). The Mexican girl's cutting her hair "when young women's hair is a glorious adornment," to accelerate her Latin studies, contrasts with the North African's famed lack of sexual restraint. Augustine complains that marriage would have been a legitimate channel for his passions, though a baser one than abstinence. Sor Juana's self-described "total antipathy . . . toward marriage"[14] is brought into relief by the language of passion, which portrays her devotion to learning: "great love of the truth" was "so vehement and powerful . . . that neither repression from without nor my own observations," could keep her from "following this 'natural inclination'"(OC 4:444.188–93). His passion is sexual; hers, intellectual.

PAUL'S VOCATION

SOR JUANA'S CHOICE of Paul as a voice through whom she speaks is another example of her acumen and ingenuity, another example of her "equivocal intentionality."[15] She does this even though, or perhaps, because of the very fact that he is the authority used to justify the silencing of women. Whereas the narrative of her early life is meant to establish that she is unlike (and better than) Augustine, the tissue of textual referents she establishes linking her to Paul— the most autobiographical of all the New Testament writers— emphasizes their similarities. Within the broader framework of his life, there is one major parallel worth noting. Paul's speaking in the name of Christ was frequently called into question because of his history: He was a known persecutor of Christians before his conversion, leaving open suspicions that his conversion was not genuine. Sor Juana's own continued connections with the court, her secular poetry and drama, left her open to the charge that the bishop of

Puebla leveled against her: She had not truly undergone the necessary conversion, the true turning from the world demanded by her status as a religious.

In her opening justification of her decision to respond to the bishop, she breaks into praise of God: "Blessed are you, Lord! Not only did you refrain from giving over to the hands of another creature, not even my own, power of judgment over me . . . but you reserved it for your mercy, because you love me more than I can love myself" (OC 4:441.58–66). Then, immediately begging the bishop/Philotea's pardon for this "digression which was ravished from her by the force of truth" (OC 4:441.67–68), she commences to explain her movement from silence into speech. Rhetorically, this achieves two things: It is the beginning of a complex of citations from 2 Cor 12, which reinforces her connection to Paul and, because it introduces her movement from silence to speech, resonates with another generally known detail of Paul's life from 2 Cor 10. Though a brilliant letter writer, he was a poor speaker (*sermo contemptibilis*) with an unimpressive physical presence (*praesentia autem corporis infirma*). The power which God has given him is to build up, not to tear down, he writes, and he does not intend to intimidate (Latin *terrere*) the community with his letters. Sor Juana is also a "writer of letters," among them the *Letter* in which she did not intend to "intimidate" anyone. Her *physical presence* (*praesentia corporis*) reveals her as a woman, thus, by definition, not only unimpressive as a public speaker, but so contemptible (*contemptibilis*) that speech is officially denied her.

Ten lines later in a composite of Acts 9:15 and 2 Cor 12:2,4, which designate Paul a "sacred vessel of election" (a feminine metaphor for the masculine Paul), the nun again cites the Latin of the Vulgate (2 Cor 12:4): He was "ravished to the third heaven" into a mystical state that defies definition: "Whether in the body or out of the body, I do not know. God knows." Sor Juana has also been ravished, "ravished by the force (*fuerza*) of truth" (OC 4:441.68). Whereas Paul heard the most holy secrets of God (*audivit arcana Dei*), which it is impermissible for humans to speak (*quae non licet homini loqui*)(OC 4:442.76), Sor Juana, the reader may infer, is not permitted to speak of what she has learned through the great gift of love of learning that God has given her.

Yet she does speak (OC 4:444.183–84). Like Paul, she is torn in another direction by the pressure of the community to bring her gifts into the open. Paul speaks of his reluctance to "boast" (*glori-arse*) of his gifts and of being "driven" or forced by his enemies to do so: "*Vos me cogistis*" (You have forced me) (2 Cor 12:1–12). Sor Juana repeats: "In truth, I have never written, except when "*violen-tada y forzada*" (OC 4:444.168), which Trueblood translates, "pressured and forced,"[16] but as both words can mean "rape" in Spanish, they underscore the Bishop's violation of her will not to have the *Letter* published. This impression is only reinforced by her protest that "I have never written of my own free will, except when *forced* by another." Coming immediately before the Latin citation "*Vos me cogistis*" (You have forced me), it again strengthens the metaphor of sexual violation.

Other close textual parallels to 2 Cor 12 underscore the connection. Paul: "was caught up as far as the third heaven" (2 Cor 12:2). "Whether in the body or out of the body . . . I do not know, God knows" (2 Cor 12:2–3) (*nescio, Deus sit*). Sor Juana writes: "His Majesty knows why and for what reason" (*sabe por qué y para qué*) (OC 4: 444.193–94) he has given her the inextinguishable inclination to learning. Paul has a thorn in the flesh, the angel of Satan sent by God "to buffet" or "torment" him to keep him from being "unduly elevated by the magnificence of such revelations" (*Et ne magnitudo revelatione extollat me*) (2 Cor 12:7). Sor Juana: "God in his mercy gave me the great grace of love of truth . . . which neither the oppression of others nor my own reflection could repress" (OC 4:444.187–90). Paul begs God three times that "the messenger of Satan" be taken from him (2 Cor 12:8). Sor Juana's "thorn in the flesh" *is* her love of learning, and she begs God "to extinguish the light of her reason, leaving only enough to guard his Law, because the rest was superfluous, according to some, *for a woman* there are even those who say that it harms them" (OC 4: 444.193–97).

As if again to emphasize her tie to the apostle, the nun ends with a passage textually very close to Rom 7:24: "Wretched creature that I am, who is there to rescue me from this state of death? Who but God? Thanks be to him through Jesus Christ our Lord! To sum up then: Left to myself I serve God's law with my mind, but with my unspiritual nature I serve the law of sin." Sor Juana concludes with this variation: "I thought that I was fleeing from myself, but, wretch that I am, I carried myself with me, and I carried my greatest enemy in this inclination which I do not know whether to consider gift or punishment that Heaven has given me" (OC 4:447.283–86). For Paul, *flesh* was evil and *mind* was good. For Sor Juana, the dilemma was more subtle; she was ready to give up the flesh—sensual pleasures, matrimony, companionship—but it is her mind that seems driven with an appetite, which, according to the bishop, is sinful.

Socrates' Apology

Though Sor Juana does not mention Socrates by name in the *Response*, his famous *Apologia*, or "defense," as well as his figure, emerge as her own defense assumes characteristics obviously "socratic."[17] Just as Socrates is known for his ironic mode of argument, the *Response* is acknowledged as "fundamentally ironic" in one scholar's demonstration of Sor Juana's expert orchestration of multi-levelled irony.[18] Like Socrates, who claims he cannot be accused of teaching because his only knowledge is of what he does not know,[19] Sor Juana maintains she studies, not in order to teach, but "only in order to see, if by studying, I would become less ignorant" (OC 4:444.180–82). Like Socrates, who declares he is persecuted because of his search for the truth by "examining myself and others,"[20] Sor Juana, at several points, protests that she is persecuted, not for knowledge, because she does not know ("*no el saber que aún no sé*"), but for her love of learning (OC 4:451.467). "In all I am saying, venerable Lady, I do not mean that I have been persecuted for being learned, only for my love of learning and letters, not because I have been successful in either" (OC 4:450.710–14)[21] Later, she reminds the reader that the Athenians (who thought themselves the only civilized people, all others being barbarians) had the "barbarous" law of exiling those who excel, as an example of a perennial societal attitude: "So it is today, and so it has always been" (OC 4:453.533–41). Luis Cortest, in his article on Sor Juana's philosophy, remarks on the appropriateness of this "return to Athens . . . the site of the first great crime committed against philosophy,"[22] the condemnation and death of Socrates, the most celebrated victim of this law.

A corollary of Sor Juana's choice of Paul, the beleaguered apostle, and Socrates, the indicted sage, is their strong connection to both pagan and Christian worlds. This was an issue for the nun, because literary education was primarily of the Greek and Latin pagan classics, and because the bishop's challenge was to her literary activities. Paul, though he can claim to be the most Jewish of

Jews, a Pharisee who had studied with Hillel, is not only the "apostle to the Gentiles" (Acts 26:17, 28:28), but a master of the Greek language who had studied the Greek philosophers, as Sor Juana points out in a later section (OC 4:470.1240–45). Socrates was "baptized" into the Christian tradition by later admirers,[23] a tradition to which Sor Juana referred ten years earlier in her letter to Núñez: "What Christian is not ashamed of being wrathful in view of the patience of a pagan Socrates?"[24]

Through her suggested links with Socrates, Paul, and Augustine, Sor Juana has associated herself with the masculine tradition of thought and reflection. Later in the autobiographical sections of the *Response,* she justifies her right to be an intellectual woman based on a tradition of learned women, illustrating that "women writing . . . are not, then, *inside* and *outside* of the male tradition; they are inside two traditions simultaneously."[25]

SOR JUANA'S IMITATIO CHRISTI

"USE YOUR GREAT talents to paint a portrait of the Lord that would at the same time enflame your heart with love for him" (OC 4: 457.696). Fernández de Santa Cruz's recommendation to Sor Juana reflected a standard spirituality popularized in Thomas à Kempis's *Imitation of Christ* that idealized "the way of the cross" as the path of patient suffering and flight from the world and its values.[26] The nun responds by conforming to the letter of the bishop's request while circumventing its restrictive spirit.[27] Again through a complex network of images, she suggests that the response of Christ's followers differs according to their individual personality and situation. Sor Juana anticipates, without explicitly formulating it, the comment of Albert Schweitzer on his century's "life of Jesus" investigations: Each theologian's portrait of Jesus reflected as much of the writer himself as that of Jesus. Thus when she depicts Jesus as Divine Beauty, calling forth love in those who contemplate him, she has projected him into the realm of the aesthetic, which is also central to her life as an artist. By portraying him as a "maker of signs," she connects him with her own activity as an author. When she presents Jesus as Wisdom Incarnate, she also points out that he was condemned for his wisdom (as she is).

CHRIST AS BEAUTY INCARNATE

"WHAT MORE LOVABLE endowment than that of divine beauty?" (OC 4:453.545). Sor Juana's first question about Jesus in the *Response* reflects how much beauty, as a christological trait, was on her mind in 1690, the year which also saw the publication in Mexico of her play *El Divino Narciso*, in which Christ is the beautiful Narcissus who dies for love of his "image," human nature. This arresting Christological image has been a magnet for biographers of Sor Juana since Ludwig Pfandl's Freudian analysis of the Mexican nun in the 1940s, which saw it as her attempt to resolve her own narcissism.[28] More recently, Stephanie Merrim has drawn connections between what she develops as Sor Juana's literary configuration of herself in the *Response* and her conscious (?) self-portrait as Christ in *The Divine Narcissus*.[29]

In Sor Juana's sacramental drama, *El Divino Narciso*, Ovid's arrogant hunter, Narcissus, has become the God of whom the mystics speak, who is no longer king, but suffering lover. She draws from the writings of the great Carmelite mystics, John of the Cross and Teresa of Ávila, to enrich her idea by reversing their imagery. For example, in one of Teresa of Ávila's poems, God, the gentle hunter pierces her soul with a poisoned dart of love, which unites her to her Creator, who is "my lover for me and I am for my lover."[30] Similarly, John of the Cross has the bride refer to the wounds the hunter has made in the heart of the beloved.[31] Sor Juana has Divine Narcissus wounded rather than inflicting wounds. The arrows of love have so painfully wounded him that he will die for love (OC 3:78.1694–96).

Because the bishop demanded: "I would wish that you imitate . . . Saint Teresa, not by writing poetry, but also in your choice of subject,"[32] Sor Juana reminds him that "the holy mother and my mother Teresa" (OC 4:453.566) said, that after she had beheld the beauty of Jesus, she lost all attraction to earthly beauty. What, she asks, as she begins her section on Jesus in her opening questions, could have been the cause of the hatred of the Pharisees, given the divine beauty of Jesus? Through a series of rhetorical questions, she develops characteristics of this beauty in images, recalling those in Teresa's *Interior Castle*, where a central metaphor for the soul is a castle of very clear crystal which houses in its center the "sun," God himself.[33] The Mexican nun describes the beauty of Christ's face as a clear crystal through which the rays of divinity emanate. She depicts divine beauty as "enrapturing" hearts, using the Spanish *arrebatar* (rapture), suggesting one of the later phases of mystical prayer in the Carmelite's work.[34] Teresa sees the state of rapture at the beauty of Christ as being beyond all human will.[35] According to Sor Juana, Christ's divine beauty has the power to subject human wills, as does human beauty.

JESUS THE MAKER OF SIGNS

SOR JUANA'S ASTONISHMENT at the Pharisees' immunity to the beauty of Jesus serves to bring into high relief the reason for their hatred as they ask (OC 4:454.579): "*Quid facimus, qui hic homo multa signa facit?*" "This man is performing many signs . . . and what action are we taking?" (Jn 11:47). Sor Juana chooses to translate *signo* (sign) rather than *milagro* (miracle) as part of a web of connections she has already begun weaving, by using variations of the word *sign*, one of which is to consistently use *señalarse* rather than *distinguirse* for *excel*. Her experiences with her own "unfortunate" talent for writing verses (OC 4:452.524–25) leads her to conclude that the person who excels (*se señala*), or whom God endows with excellence (*le señala Dios*), will be considered an enemy of the common good, as was the case in democratic Athens, and as Machiavelli maintained. In the paragraph beginning with Jn 11:47 she initiates her word game. Jesus is the one who is persecuted for making many signs (again the Latin: *multa signa facit*). "Good God! That doing something *señalada* could be the cause of one's death!" This expression *multa signa facit* (she repeats for the third time), hearkens back to the prophetic claims that the messiah "of the "root of Jesse . . . shall be a sign for the people" (Is 11:10), as well as "a sign of contradiction" (Lk 2:34) (OC 4:454.595). Again she asks: "Because of a sign? (*signo*) He dies! Designated? (*señalado*) Then let him suffer since that is the reward of one who excels (*se señala*)" (OC 4:545.597–98). By combining, the nun has used the term to hammer her identity to that of Jesus in his unjust suffering. She is the one who is *señalada* in the opening, because of her poetic gifts, and has suffered as a result. The expression *multa signa facit* is also translated as who does or performs many signs, but a literal rendering *could* read who "makes many signs." Sor Juana, as a writer, is also a maker of signs.

JESUS AS DIVINE WISDOM

JUST AS HER concern for the arts leads Sor Juana to focus on the beauty of Christ, so her passion for the life of the mind directs her toward development of the figure of Christ as Divine Wisdom. Wisdom's place of honor in society, she maintains, is more fragile than that of power or wealth, which have the means to defend their prestige from attack. Furthermore, she contends, citing Gracian, because intelligence is what distinguishes different degrees of being—angels from humans, humans from animals—people are more sensitive to something which seems to counter, or place in a diminished light, their own intelligence (OC 4:455.116). The biblical scenes which Sor Juana selects for her portrait are all connected with phases of the trial of Jesus, rather than those which emphasize physical suffering, such as whipping, carrying the cross, his actual crucifixion. Each presents Jesus in a situation of suffering because of the ignorance of those around him. Each scene is fraught with the ambiguity and tenuous nature of human knowing. What the actors in each scene think they know, or think they are doing is not what we know they are really doing. In commenting on the scene in which the Pharisees seek to destroy Jesus as "maker of signs" or "miracle worker," Sor Juana asks, "Why does someone who 'makes signs' or works miracles deserve to die?" Hardly a reason to kill someone, she observes dryly, adding: "If they had said he was an instigator of riots, a subversive they would have been lying." This direct contradiction of the truth would have been too blatant for such "learned" men as the Pharisees. It is the conclusion they draw from the fact, not the fact itself which is in contradiction to their reason (OC 4:454.585–87). In another aside, the nun observes that learned men, when they are carried away by their passions are prone to such inconsistencies (OC 4:454.585–87).

The second scene the nun considers is of the Roman soldiers mocking Jesus as king by placing an old purple cloak over his shoulders, a hollow reed as a scepter in his hand, and a crown of thorns on his head. Jesus is really a king, so the soldiers' crowning of him corresponds to what is actually the case, albeit, unknown to them. Even the material of the crown, the thorns, is appropriate to the secret and true significance of Jesus' death. Here Sor Juana uses military imagery, reminiscent of the Ignatian exercises: Like a victorious general, Jesus has lifted the siege that "the Prince of Darkness" has laid to the "city of the world." According to Roman custom, the appropriate crown in this case is not gold or silver but that of the natural products of "the field of battle" from whence the siege has been lifted. Jesus' triumphal procession is that of the weeping women because "the triumph of the wise is obtained through suffering and celebrated with weeping" (OC 4:456.671–73). Given the example of Christ, his followers who seek wisdom can expect no other crown.

In a third scene, Peter is in the courtyard of the chief priest waiting the outcome of Jesus' hearing when he denies knowing him. By this point Sor Juana has fully allegorized, or hypostacized Jesus as "Wisdom." In a rather daring comparison, as she says, Peter is the "prince of the apostles," and the nun likens herself to him. The nun argues, in effect, that if Peter can cut such a poor figure and still be admired as "prince of the apostles," her own love of wisdom must be admissible. She uses two quotations from the scene of his denial as proofs that Peter, although ignorant and following wisdom from afar (*a longe*) (OC 4:457.728), was destined to be persecuted for being a lover of wisdom (*amoroso de la sabiduría*) (OC 4:457.727). Though Peter denies knowing Jesus both to the serving maid and the man in the courtyard,[36] for simply being with Jesus ("*Et hic cum illo erat*") he is open to persecution. By ending her recapitulation of this scene with an image recalling the three young men placed in the fiery furnace by the despotic king Nebuchadnezzar (Daniel 3:3), she reinforces the idea that the search for wisdom brings suffering and demands courage. Her desire to follow Jesus (Wisdom) has only resulted in "bringing me nearer to the fire of persecution, to the furnace of torments" and led even to her being prohibited from studying (OC 4:458.735).

DIVINE WISDOM AND HOLY IGNORANCE

IN ANSWER TO the reproach of "her greatest enemies," those who "love her and desire her good" (OC 4:450.516), she initially concedes that her study was not appropriate for the "holy ignorance" to which she was bound by her religious vows. However, she soon undermines her concession by setting herself in scenes where she is with those considered ignorant or crazy. Amy Oliver has spoken of the various levels of irony in Sor Juana, and in the *Response* she uses its many distinct forms. Here irony consists in the contrast of what is stated and what is implied. Stated is that she is "crazy," as she subtly demonstrates her erudition and her learning. In her description of her learning principles of chemistry and physics while watching eggs fry, she develops a parody of learning, even though it may refer to something that really happened and by so doing she makes herself into a clown or fool. Her parody begins with the rather coy: "What could I tell you of secrets of nature which I have discovered while cooking?"(OC 4:459.800–801). She knows that such things are trivial, but utilizes them in order to reveal herself fully. "I think this will cause you to laugh, but, Lady, what can women know, but kitchen philosophy?" Her follow-up, "If Aristotle had cooked, he would have written much more," presents the reader with the hilarious image of the great sage of antiquity standing over a hot stove (OC 4:460.115–16).

The nun continues her caricature of herself by describing how doctors, who prescribed she stop studying during an illness, were forced to reconsider after several days because "so strong and vehement were my cogitations that they devoured more spirits in a quarter hour than four days' study of books"(OC 4:460.821–24).[37] Even sleep does not quiet her obsession, but, contrary to what one might expect, represents the time when with greater clarity her mind continues to argue and make verses. Though this is obviously a reference to her beloved poem *First Dream*, the only work she claims to have written without constraint, it also is a reference to the realm of the mind associated with dreams, the irrational, prophecy, illusion, and irreality.

One way of associating herself with the "ignorant," is through her association with children. Though it is impossible to show that Sor Juana had read the biography of another genius and child prodigy of her century, Blaise Pascal, parallels in her text and that of Pascal's biography by his sister are striking. Pascal's father, a mathematician himself, forbade him the study of mathematics because he felt the boy's natural fascination with it would take away from his studying more important subjects, such as Latin. In Sor Juana's case her "spiritual fathers" (the bishop and others), tried to discourage her from using her God-given intellectual abilities and literary talents to devote herself to prayer and contemplation. In spite of his father's prohibitions, Pascal's mathematical genius could not be stiffled. Observing the twelve-year-old Blaise tracing geometric figures with coal on the tiles in front of a fireplace, he was astounded to see that on his own, his son had arrived at Euclid's thirty second principle.[38] Sor Juana's examples of her own mental activity during the period when study was forbidden her offer similarities to Pascal's story and his mathematical interests. She describes herself walking in front of a fireplace in a large dormitory and noticing that, contrary to measurable fact, the lines of the room appeared not to be running parallel, but inclined toward each other. This caused her to wonder whether this might have been the reason that the ancients doubted that the earth was round. Her next example suggests the young Pascal's essay on the mathematics of the cone, written by the sixteen-year-old in 1639–40.[39] Sor Juana describes herself noticing the movement of a top with which some girls were playing. "In my craziness," she recounts (OC 4:459.779), she had flour brought and sifted on the floor, in order to observe the path the top traced as it slowed to a stop, thereby suggesting an interest in the shape that fascinated the young Pascal.

All her intellectual activity as described above would have been considered "merits" ("as I have seen them celebrated as such in men"), she maintains, but with her, they are not because they operate out of necessity and not of her own free will. Though she avoids saying that her talent is not considered "meritorious" because of her being a woman, it is clearly implied. Once more, her tactic is to present herself as a child in the matter of intellect. As a result, she cannot be credited, nor censured since moral responsibility, comes, according to church doctrine, at the age of seven, the "age of reason" after which children were considered elligible for the sacrament of confession. The reader, however, knows from the nun's earlier description of herself as a child, her deliberate, one might say willful, learning to read, her asceticism (cutting her hair in order to motivate herself to greater efforts in learning), that, even as a child, her will was operative. Here is another instance of an irony created against the background of a previous text within Sor Juana's own "apologia," emphasized by her closing of this section, in which she writes that she "lives contantly with no confidence in herself, not trusting her judgment in one thing or another." She submits herself to the judgment of Sor Philotea, adding "after all, this has merely been a simple narration of my inclination toward literature" (OC 4:460.840–45). Again, obvious irony. This presentation has been anything but simple.

9

In Countless Numbers: The Tradition of Learned Women

I tried to elevate these studies to the service of God, because the final goal to which I aspired was to study theology, and it seemed a disgraceful incompetence, in as far as I was a Catholic, not to know everything which can be attained by natural means of the divine mysteries.

(OC 4:447.300–305)

SOR JUANA HAD insisted on her natural, uncontrolable drive to learn and contrasted it with her appropriately humble assessment of her own piety: "O if it had been for love of God, which would have been proper, how much merit I would have gained!" (OC 4:447.297–99). *Merit* is a key term, since the Catholic theology of justification (opposed to grace alone in Protestant theology), becomes a stepping stone for her "justification" of her studies; also implied is another principle of classical Catholic doctrine: "grace builds on nature,"[1] which is the theological basis for Sor Juana's theory of the interconnectedness of all knowledge and experience in the life of the knowing subject.

SOR JUANA'S THEOLOGICAL PATH

THOUGH SOR JUANA opens her discussion of theological method with the hierarchical image of the ladder or staircase (OC 4:447.831), when she describes her own course of study she maintains it does not

depend on the order of one thing over another, but on her interest in everything "in general." Her studies have been largely
dependent upon the books which chance brought into her hands.
As a result, she has a basic knowledge of numerous disciplines
without what might be considered expertise in one. What might
seem a drawback in disciplines requiring manual skills, such as the
playing of a musical instrument, is an advantage in the area of
speculative thinking.

The nun's reasons for not having devoted more time to the
study of theology proper lead her naturally to discuss her experience of study formed to a great extent by the social limitations of
her gender: she could not attend institutes of learning; she was left
"to read and read further, to study and more study with no other
teacher than the books" with their "characters without soul, lacking
the living voice of a teacher" (OC 4:447.291–95). Sor Juana is not
motivated by skepticism toward deeper learning, but by enthusiasm. There is always more to be learned. Similarly, she does not
emphasize the contradictory nature of the individual disciplines,
but their complementarity. She seeks to persuade everyone from her
own experience that the wide range of her studies helps rather than
hinders the intellect—"bringing light and opening paths" to one
another from the interlocking nature of all wisdom. "All things
issue from God who is at the same time center and circumference
from which all things come and where all the lines of creation come
to a halt"(OC 4:450.421–24).

Though complaining of the distractions of convent life, Sor
Juana sees learning ideally as a communal undertaking and regrets
on more than one occasion not only the lack of a living teacher,
but also fellow students (*condiscípulos*). Her teacher has been a
mute book, her fellow student, the inkwell (OC 4: 450.441–45).
She seeks the company of the learned, which she does not find,
and she disciplines herself to avoid the natural companionship of
her sisters by making a vow only to enter the cell of another if
forced to by obedience or charity (OC 4: 452.487–92). As a result
of her atypical learning environment, she can bring a type of objec-
tivity divorced from the normal social conditioning imposed by
formal schooling.

In fact, Sor Juana maintains that God intended creation to be
his book, and desires that it be read and interpreted. "There is no
creature no matter how lowly in which the activity of the creator is

not recognizable. There is not one creature that is not a source of astonishment to those who consider it as they should" (OC 4: 458.747–49). This is the primary logic of her argument, but even here it is part of another underlying structure of the passage: the correspondence between the "natural," "bookless" learning and the division of the sciences.[2] Sor Juana introduces this in what appears to be a random series of observations stimulated by the convent environment around her. She observes the shadow on the walls of the convent dormitory. She watches young girls at play. She cooks. She sleeps. As a result, in an apparently casual manner her daily routine brings her into contact with all the sciences and demonstrates the interrelatedness of academic disciplines and human experience. Her references to creation signals theology, her questioning the various types of persons she encounters, philosophy/psychology. Geometry, optics, and cosmology are all implicit in her observations of the shadows on the dormitory wall. Her comments on her manner of knowing point to an awareness of classical and contemporary epistemology. Her observations of girls playing with a top, geometry and physics, and their playing a type of pickup sticks—music, theology, and esoteric literature.

In as far as the Sacred Book reflects the world, a theologian needs to be knowledgeable in all the disciplines of the world. In what seems to be a consistent rhetorical device, in order to avoid the imperative, or to seem to be "legislating," Sor Juana uses the interrogative throughout the long listing of the many sciences and arts which she is arguing are necessary to theological understanding. This series of questions begins: "How to understand style (method) of the Queen of the Sciences without knowing the style of the handmaids? How, without logic, could I know the general and specific methods used in writing Sacred Scripture? How, without rhetoric, understand her figures, tropes and expressions?" How, without physics, music, arithmetic, geometry, architecture, law, profane history, the Holy Fathers, music and astrology, "only to mention the noble sciences, not the mechanical ones which are also necessary, can one penetrate the sacred mysteries?" The Bible, as "the book which includes all books, and the science in which all the sciences are included" (OC 4: 449.372–75), also needs prayer and a virtuous life, "purgation of soul and illumination of the mind" (OC 4:449.381–83) as a prerequisite for its study.

Though Sor Juana uses the idea of the interrelationship of knowledge as justification for her interest in worldly studies and stresses the interlocking nature of all disciplines, in fact her primary emphasis is on exegesis as the basis of theology proper. In her own theological writings there is no reference to magisterial statements, and church fathers are cited as aids to helping understand "the obscure expression of the prophets"(OC 4:448.354). To the extent that theology is textual analysis it is tied to rhetoric, and also to poetry, which we are aware Sor Juana considers her forte. She recalls the widespread praise of those who have used poetry for religious expression: the sibyls, the Prophets, King David, Moses in his canticle, Solomon in the Song of Songs, Jeremiah in Lamentations. Paul incorporates pagan poetry into two of his letters, showing that he was acquainted with pagan verse and used it in his compositions. Augustine was known to have defended poetry in *Wisdom of Solomon* 11:21. The final, and most exalted example is that of "the Queen of Wisdom, Our Lady" who intoned the Magnificat in verse. It is not the fault of poetry that it has its bad practitioners. Like any other discipline it can be put to good use or ill.[3]

Tradition of Learned Women

Though Sor Juana builds connections between herself and major figures of the Christian intellectual tradition to a large extent by way of contrast, she is also conscious of building a *bridge* between the tradition of learning of men and that of women. In this context she uses her being "of an ecclesiastical state," i.e., as a professed nun as a justification for her pursuit of learning, deliberately ignoring the fact that canon law considered the non-ordained religious technically as *laity* (OC 4:447.305). Furthermore, the scholarly tradition of learning of her own order has not only Saint Jerome as a model, but also Saint Paula (the patron saint of Sor Juana's convent). It would be disgraceful, she maintains, "to be an idiot daughter of such learned parents" (OC 4:447.306–8).

Moreover, her study has shown her that she is part of a tradition of learned women. To prove this she begins enumerating a long list of outstanding women, from the Bible, from pagan antiquity, from early Christianity, and among her contemporaries. She makes it clear that she is not the first to make such lists, adding that there are many she omits to mention, "so as not to copy what others have said (a vice I have always hated)" (OC 4:462.902). She begins with women from the Old Testament: Deborah, the Queen of Sheba, Abigail, Esther, Rahab, and Anna whom she praises for leadership qualities in government, wisdom, persuasion, piety, and perseverance. "And an infinite number more with other types of qualities and virtues" (OC 4:461.858–60). This hyperbole can be seen as a device to universalize the capacity for extraordinary virtue and learning in women based on *the* authoritative source, the Bible.

The *classical* tradition, another authoritative source for education, also presents *countless* outstanding women. The nun's list of pagan women begins with the Sibyls, the divinely inspired prophetesses which Christian antiquity assumed as legitimate, and Minerva, assumed to have been a very wise woman and, therefore, divinized, and proceeds with matrons, teachers, philosophers, rhetoricians, and astrologers. Once more she ends with the refrain: "And a host of others who merit being named, Greeks, muses, oracles; all of them no less than learned women celebrated and venerated in antiquity as such, without mentioning another infinite number of whom books are full" (OC 4:461.881).

Although fewer women in early Christianity are named, they are praised with a vehemence that verges on the grotesque; of Paula, student of Jerome, Sor Juana quotes St. Jerome: "If all the limbs of my body were tongues, they would not suffice to publish, make known the wisdom and virtue of Paula" (OC: 4:461.892). The strangest must be the Roman Proba Falconia, a fourth century prodigy who "wrote an elegant book of the mystery of our holy faith (actually a history of the Old and New Testaments) composed of verses of Virgil" (OC 4:462.898). Perhaps this example indicates that the bizarre is also not absent from women of learning. Fewer still are the contemporary women named, but that is because others have named them, she maintains.

In addition to constructing an alternative tradition of learned women, Sor Juana reveals the negative aspects of the male tradition. Whereas only women who are gifted should be teachers, the same is true for men, she argues. "Many men, merely because they are men, think that they are *sabios* (learned)" (OC 4:462.928). Sometimes the more stupid they are, the more they presume to know. To parallel her list of famous learned women she then lists male heretics: Pelagius; Arius; Luther; a contemporary, Cazalla. For such as these, allowing them to study was "like putting a sword in the hands of a madman. The instrument, as such good for defense, in their hands leads to their death and the death of many others" (OC 4:463.949). Quoting Rom 12:3, she argues that men who are not qualified also should be silent in the church. She, herself, no matter how much she studied could never know as much as Aristotle or St. Augustine because she is not endowed as they.

WOMEN'S EDUCATION

EVIDENCE OF AN alternative tradition of learned women of which she is a part, is also taken by Sor Juana as proof that "authoritative tradition" of the hierarchical church has sanctioned, even celebrated women of learning. After having shown that both the Bible (St. Paul) and *the* biblical scholar of the Church, Jerome (his translation had been "canonized" after the Council of Trent), support not just women learning—as Philotea/Bishop Santa Cruz will admit—but also that women teach, the nun can argue that the lack of appropriate higher education for women of her own society goes against the accepted tradition of the Church.

Sor Juana laments the grave dangers to "our republic" (OC 4: 464.1014), which could have been avoided had women been able to teach women "as St. Paul and my Father St. Jerome commanded" (OC 4:464.1016-17). Because of this prohibition male tutors are the only teachers available if a young woman's parents[4] wish her to receive more than a rudimentary education. She reminds of the damaging examples which one "experiences every day" (OC 4:465. 124) of "unequal unions" resulting from the close proximity of tutor and student. As a result, she continues, many parents prefer their daughters remain ignorant rather than "expose them to such a notorious danger as the familiar company of men" (OC 4:465.1029). This would not be a problem if, as Sor Juana repeats, as St. Paul advocated, learned women were allowed to teach, and even form a type of guild for their expertise (*magisterio*) (OC 4:465.1031) as women have done in other areas of labor.

Extending her deliberations she asks, "What objection could there be to such women teaching?" (OC 4:465.1033). She develops a picture of women's education which turns that of many of her contemporaries on its head. Her ecclesiastical superior, Manuel Aguijar y Seijas, apparently incorporated this attitude to an extreme degree. According to his admiring biographer Lezamis, "If he knew that a woman had so much as entered his house, he would have to order the bricks she had stepped on removed . . . He did not want a woman to touch anything in his house or to cook his meals. He did not want to hear them sing, or even to hear them mentioned."[5] He refused to call on the new viceroy, the Count de Galve, so as not to have to meet his wife. Such a view saw woman as the vessel of the Devil, designed to lead men into sin and perdition. (Especially dangerous to the vow of celibacy which clerics took.) All women were daughters of Eve, whose misstep was the cause of sin, suffering, and death in the world.[6] Though this portrait of Aguiar may not be accurate in all respects, the fact that it was part of his "official portrait" by an admirer shows the degree to which attitudes similar to his were approved.

One of the primary biblical supports for this was 1 Tm 2:14, (part of the same passage to which Sor Juana cites in OC 4:467. 1117) often used against women: Adam is not seduced, but the woman is deceived and seduced.[7] In context this means that woman was the weaker, able to be seduced by the devil. She in turn tempts Adam. Part of Sor Juana's intertextual play here is that the reality of life allows another interpetation of the passage. Here she paints the portrait of the modest, shy girl forced into immediacy of contact[8] with the male tutor. A signal to the subtext is the unusual Spanish word *verecunda* used to describe the young girl seated beside the tutor. Salceda deems it necessary to translate it in a footnote for his readers.[9] First Tm 2:9 when describing the proper demeanor of women uses *verecundia* (for modesty).[10] ("Women must dress in a becoming manner, modestly and soberly.") The obvious unstated premise is that it is *men* that are the cause of the lack of education of women, not women. The passage "Adam is not seduced, but the woman is deceived and seduced" (1 Tm 2:14) has received a novel interpretation in this context. Women have the ability (see the long list of wise women) and the authority (St. Paul, Jerome) to teach. In fact it is men's lechery that makes it morally imperative that women be allowed to teach women.

Women Teaching in the Church

Everyone knows, Sor Juana insists, that men can only teach women, without being dangerous, in the confessional ("in the distant decency of the pulpit"[11)] or through the remote knowledge of books. This social necessity does not mean that women should not be learned or even teach, rather it mandates that they do. Those who cite the one Pauline passage about women being silent in the church (1 Tm 2:9) to rail against (*blasfemen*)[12] women learning and teaching, do not take into account the other passage also by "the apostle," in his letter to Titus (Ti 2:4), that women be "good teachers" (*bene docentes*).

They further ignore an important source from the life of the early Church: Eusebius' *Church History*. According to Eusebius, 1 Tm 2:9 is merely asserting "that women should be silent" as a matter of politeness due to a speaker, not a rule for all times and places. Sor Juana, based on Eusebius' description, argues that 1 Tm 2:9's admonition is only correctly to be applied to this particular incident and not to be interpreted as a general rule. Building on the insight from Eusebius which demonstrated the necessity of the knowledge of history and ancient customs for proper interpretation of the Bible, Sor Juana enumerates a series of additional examples "incidentally" connected with women: the custom of care for the widows, an interpretation of the "the valiant woman" in Prv 31, and the Gospel scene in which Christ reprimands the Pharisee who invited him to dine, for not having given him the reception normally afforded a guest. This same scene has the appearance of the unnamed woman who anoints Jesus and washes his feet, though Sor Juana does not mention this part of the example. However, it is a scene in which a woman rather than a male leader of the community knows more about Jesus, and what appropriate response to him is.

Sor Juana continues her own analysis of 1 Cor 14:34 and 1 Tm 2:11 by moving beyond an immediate literal understanding to one that seeks to see the text in an expanded view of what Church is. Though "grammar" is important for the proper understanding of texts, their full meaning extends beyond the scope of what some "mere grammarians" (OC 4:467.1113) may admit. The passage "Women shall be silent in the Church" (1 Cor 14:34) needs to be understood in the context of other passages referring to the believing community, such as references to the people of Israel. Passages such as "*Audi Israel, et tace*" (Listen Israel, and be silent) are intended, she reiterates, to apply to a particular group in a specific situation, not to be interpreted as a general rule. Obviously, just because a group is admonished to be silent in a particular situation does not mean that they should always be silent.

Similarly reflecting on the *ecclesia* of 1 Cor 14:34 where women are admonished to silence, Sor Juana asks whether it means during services in the church building, or in the "universality of the faithful, which is the Church." To interpret the text to apply to the universality of the faithful would be to ignore the evidence of tradition, or history which reveals a long line of women who have studied and taught through their writings. Women saints such as Gertrude, Teresa, and Bridgit are obvious examples. But many have taught without the official designation of "saint," such as followers and disciples of Jesus in his time: Martha, Mary, Mary the mother of Jacob, Salome, as well as those women in the primitive church who learned from Jesus and the apostles, and taught others. The contemporary church allows even women who are not saints, such as María de Jesus de Agreda, and María de la Antigua, to write. Then in another of her wonderful asides: "neither were Saint Teresa or the others (saints canonized) during the time in which they wrote" (OC 4:468.1148).

Not only can Sor Juana place herself in a long line of *exempla*, she also interprets her own local Catholic/Christian tradition as one which makes a place for learned women. Her authority in this case is the Mexican "venerable Doctor Arce" (Juan Díaz de Arce, d. 1653), who interpreted the Pauline caution that women should be silent in the church as pertaining only to teaching publicly and preaching in the assembly. She returns "to our Arce" for examples of women of learning in Mexico. One knew the breviary by heart, so that on any occasion she had a quote ready to hand. The other was so familiar with the letters of Jerome that Arce wrote: "It seemed to me that I was hearing Jerome in Spanish." Arce felt it was a great pity that these two talented women had not had "a better course of study with scientific principles" (OC 4:469.1210). Similarly, Sor Juana claims, Sor Philotea has been urging her to do the same. Another level of irony returns as the nun deliberately misinterprets the bishop's admonition to "change the books of your ruin into the book of Jesus Christ" (OC 4:695) into an encouragement for her to pursue higher theological studies.

Even publication of her own "teaching" work, the *Athenagoric Letter*, proves that women may legitimately write in the church. Against unnamed detractors she asks if it was a crime simply to relate her opinion "with all due permission of our Holy Mother Church" (OC 4:468.1168). She did nothing different from Vieira, and her work passed official censorship. Her highest aspiration is to be known as a "Catholic and obedient daughter, of my Holy Mother Church" (OC 4:469.1186). She concludes with a supposition which obviously some of her detractors did not accept: "As I was free to dissent from Vieira, so is anyone to dissent from my opinion" (OC 4:469.1190–92).

THE DESTINY OF HER "CHILD"

THOUGH IN HER primary level of presentation Sor Juana is writing about what tools are necessary for interpretation of a Biblical text, the same methods apply, she assures us, to pagan texts. By implication, the same things are true about *any text*, and we can also surmise they are meant to apply to the text *she* is writing (OC 4: 1060–1111). In *her* text the reader may expect to find double meanings of words such as the type she mentions in Martial. In *her* text we might expect to find "putting feminine for the masculine" (OC 4: 467.1109–10), which we do in terms of *señora* for *señor* (the bishop). In *her* text we might expect to be aware of switching from second to third voice (OC 4:467.1106), which we do as she apologizes in her closing for "using the familiar *vos*" instead of the "grammatically third person" *usted*. In *her* text a "knowledge of customs" might be necessary. Just as a correct interpretation of "Women should be silent in the Church"(1 Cor 14:34) requires moving beyond the immediacy of the printed text to the larger context of what has actually been practiced in the Church, so an adequate understanding of the *Response*, must also look to a larger context. Much of the larger context of the seventeenth-century ecclesiastical society has been lost to us. Therefore, caution is necessary when making assumptions about the degree to which ecclesiastical politics were behind both the publication of the *Letter* and Sor Philotea's letter. Yet if one steps back and looks at certain pieces in the mosaic that is the *Response*, it is possible to see a number of allusions to the oppressive power of Aguiar y Seijas, and this especially in the two major images of the final pages: the infant Moses, and the procession of the Roman conquerers.

Whereas the closing metaphor for her text, the *Letter*, is an embryo (*embryon*) (OC 4:434.904), her closing reference in the *Response* to the fate of her text, the *Letter*, is bound with ferocity to Moses, the leader of the Israelites from exile to freedom, who survived to adulthood only because of the intervention of a series of women.

I think had I been able to predict the fortunate destiny to which it (the *Letter*) was born, when I cast it to be exposed on the waters of the Nile of silence, where a princess like you would find it and cherish it. I believe, I repeat, that if I had thought such thing, I would have strangled it with my own hands at its birth, for fear that the clumsy scribblings of my ignorance would have appeared before the light of your knowledge (OC 4:471. 1273–79)

Once more the nun uses a biblical text to highlight the dilemma of women teaching/writing, again on two levels: one general and one relative to her own particular situation. Sor Juana clearly anticipates the interpretations of contemporary biblical scholars' attention to the dimensions of the role of women in the life of the great leader of the Israelites. In the opening of the book of Exodus, the Israelites in Egypt are no longer favored as they were in the time of Joseph, but oppressed with slave labor, *because* Pharaoh worries that they will "become too strong for us. We must take steps to ensure that they increase no further; otherwise we shall find that, if war comes, they will side with the enemy, fight against us, and become masters of the country" (Ex 1:9–10). Because of their fecundity, they are to be suppressed with degrading work for the state, and finally, when this does not suffice, an edict goes out to all Hebrew midwives to kill all male children at their birth. Sor Juana's pharoah, the forces behind Philotea, are requiring she kill her "male child" the *Letter*. Philotea is the "daughter" of this oppressive king. Santa Cruz as Bishop of Puebla is of lesser rank than Aguiar, who is Archbishop of Mexico City. Just as Pharoah's daughter gave Moses the name meaning "I drew him out of the water" (Ex 2:10) (*Quia de aqua tuli eum*), the bishop of Puebla has given a name of his own choosing (*Athenagoric Letter*) to Sor Juana's child, which she had named *Critique of a Sermon*. Sor Juana maintains she set her child afloat on the Nile of silence. The original addressee of the *Letter* was requested to "keep silent", i.e., not publish the work. The importance of the metaphor of silence as inserted into the Moses story is corroborated by the different types of silence which Sor Juana uses. Jean Franco has alluded to the different types of silence operative in the *Response*: the silence of those who are "overwhelmed by gratitude," "silence of esoteric knowledge," and the silence of treachery.[13] There is also the silence of trust. The bishop of Puebla, like Pharoah's daughter, has drawn the *Letter* out of that silence, and moved it from anonymity into the palace of Pharoah. The "princess" has trespassed the will of Pharoah, who ordered all male children (writings by women) killed. This Moses (Sor Juana's *Letter*) then is totally dependent on the good will of the "princess," because had Pharoah had his way, it would have been killed at birth.

Moreover, Pharaoh's plan requires that women betray other women. The midwives (an image Socrates used of himself; Juana compares herself to Socrates) are asked to kill the offspring of women they are supposed to be helping. In the Church, women are asked to conform to the image the "anti-woman" group has formed of them, and suppress "the male children" (the writings of other women). The midwives pretend to try, but actually they do nothing, a typical ruse of the powerless. They say that the Hebrew women are so strong that they bear their children in the field, and when the midwife arrives, they say the child has already died. Sor Juana has repeatedly emphasized that her intellectual and literary talents are gifts of God and she must respect them. The one child (Moses), and in some sense Sor Juana herself, is representative of the many whose intellectual gifts have "been killed" once they are beyond the early phases of infancy when their intelligence can no longer be hidden. The midwives, like Socrates, are also teachers. The state tolerates the education of very young girls, but does not allow them access to higher studies. Pharoah's plan would require the midwives to turn their science, which brings life into the world, into an instrument of death. Sor Juana, who lived in a convent in which young girls were taught, must at least have been aware of the extent to which as a teacher she was forced to "betray" her students because their learning could not progress beyond a certain point. An example of this stiffling of talent are two local prodigies who spout "the fathers" from memory (OC 4:1198–1212). Sor Juana notices that Arce, defender of women, mentions them "without giving the name of either one, although he uses them to prove his point" (OC 4:1212–13).

The reason given for the disobedience of the midwives is that they are "God-fearing." Sor Juana is at pains to prove that she is appropriately fearful throughout the *Response*. This is not just a type of "humility formula," but in answer to part of Sor Philotea's reproach that she is arrogant.

RENDERING TO CAESAR

SOR JUANA ALSO uses a text from Roman history to identify her adversary. The last extended image in the *Response* (OC 4: 1328–53) is a description of Julius Caesar's triumphal entry into Rome taken from Suetonius. The triumphing captains vested in purple (bishops' colors) enter the city with defeated chieftans "*en vez de brutos*" (instead of animals) pulling their chariots. Upon his entry into Mexico City, it was customary for every bishop to have an elaborate triumphal entry into the capitol, a parade which included representatives of "the conquered nations," the Indians.[14] Archbishop Aguiar y Seijas represents the conqueror. He was a Spaniard who furthermore claimed a Roman knight of Julius Caesar's house among his ancestors. The warning from Suetonius which the nun cites ("Beware, Romans we bring you one who is bald and adulterous") could apply to Aguiar y Seijas on another plane: He is quite bald according to his portrait. And as an example of a rhetorical device: Sor Juana had earlier called "adulterous" any kind of sin. (OC 4: 467.1110–11).

10

Fame and Fate

Not only do I give permission but I command[1] that this be printed, in order to prevent the consignment to oblivion of a woman who is the glorious ornament of this century.

        Cristoval Bañes de Salceda, written on July 15, 1691, near the end of his "Censura" of Volume II of *Obras*, Seville

How much work I have undertaken, how many difficulties I have had to suffer, how many times I have despaired, and how many other times I have desisted and begun again, because of my determination to learn, my conscience is my witness.

        Sor Juana quoting St. Jerome, the founder of her order, in her preface to the 1692 Seville edition of Volume II of *Obras* (OC 4: 440–41)

A SECOND RESPONSE

ON NOVEMBER 25, 1691, a year after the publication of her *Letter,* Sor Juana's *villancicos* for the feast of Catherine of Alexandria were performed in the southern city of Oaxaca. It is generally admitted that they represent a "second" *Response.* In the opening stanza, Sor Juana, speaking as the poet, commands the waters of the Nile, described in the *Response* "as waters of silence," to retreat. Here, "more fortunate" as they stop to view the figure of "Catherine," the Nile waters are full of waves which sound in "syllables, languages, numbers, and voices" (OC 2: 164).

In many respects the figure of Catherine of Alexandria, whose martyrdom is associated with the "Catherine wheel," was an obvious model for presentation of a defense of the role of the intellectual woman in the church. Canonized, she was public and exemplary. Furthermore, she was the patron saint of philosophers, as well as of the University of Mexico, an institution which had, in the not too distant past, celebrated the man whose work Sor Juana had criticized, the Jesuit Antonio de Vieira.[2] According to the breviary: "Catherine, a noble virgin of Alexandria, from an early age joined the study of the liberal arts to an ardent faith. In a short time she attained sanctity of life and perfection of doctrine, so that by her eighteenth year she surpassed all in learning."[3] As the legend continues, the tyrant Maximus, who is persecuting Christians, hears of Catherine's wisdom and summons all the wise men of Egypt to convince her of the folly of her faith. Instead, she converts them through her arguments, infuriating Maximus, who submits her to the torture of a spiked wheel. When this does not make her renounce her faith, he has her beheaded. Parallels with Sor Juana's life—such as her virginity, her interest in liberal arts (poetry), as well as her precocious learning—are apparent. Even the scene of Catherine debating the Egyptian sages has an analogue in Sor Juana's life, in her youthful debate with the scholars of her day.

Certain passages can be seen to reflect the envy of Sor Juana's public success as a woman of letters. "Because she is beautiful they envy her, in as far as she is learned they want to emulate her: O what an ancient trait to consider merits as faults"(OC 2:170).[4] Other points of contact repeat arguments in defense of women from the *Response*: Catherine "studied, argued, and taught, and it was a service to the Church, because the One who created her a rational being did not want her to remain ignorant" (OC 2:171). A chorus of peasants praise the little girl who "they say knew much, although a woman," and who "was able to convince great men"(OC 2:180).

By emphasizing a pre-Christian Egypt, Sor Juana has changed the expected frame of the saintly paradigm of the breviary's category "virgin and martyr" to an Egypt redefined in the Renaissance and seventeenth-century hermeticism as primordial source of all wisdom. Sor Juana shared with many of her contemporaries the interest in Egypt. Paz speaks of her as "yet another victim of one of the intellectual diseases of her age: Egyptomania."[5] According to connections drawn by renaissance Neoplatonists, the first and wisest philosopher was Hermes Trismegistus who could read the secret inscribings of the world's mysteries. For these writers not only was Egypt the source of all secular wisdom, it was also seen as the true bridge between Christianity and the other religions. Even a cursory presentation of major images in the eight poems reveal the importance of the non-Christian frame, as well as Sor Juana's intention to build up a *woman* as a marvel of wisdom, surpassing and summarizing in her person the seven wonders of the ancient world, the conceit of the seventh poem. Sor Juana first suggests Egypt as a source of secular and religious wisdom through her apostrophe to the river whose waters cradled Moses, the Nile. She as poet, commands them to stop their course, and though she does not say it, the reference to the Red Sea waters parting to let Moses and the Israelites pass through is clear. The waters are to stop in order to stare in amazement at Catherine, whose Gypsy beauty was augmented by virtues, surpassing those of twelve old testament heroines: Abigail, Esther, Rachel, Susanna, Deborah, Jael, Judith, Rebecca, Ruth, Bathsheba, Tamar, and Sara.

The second poem concentrates on the image of Catherine as the "Rose of Alexandria," whose flourishing colors of red (martyrdom) and white (purity) witness that "other Nile . . . which ignores beginning and has no end" (OC 2:165). Again, in a comparison with the Old Testament, Catherine's death is seen as a triumph greater than that of Judith, who beheaded the enemy commander Holofernes. Judith's triumph was to kill, Catherine's is to die. Sor Juana is careful to select an image of a martyr's death which is not suffering imposed, but chosen. She emphasizes Catherine's stance as a prudent, wise choice: "You knew" she writes, "how to acquire eternal life through a brief death"(OC 2:166).

In the third of the poems—perhaps the most dense in meaning and original in its conception—two gypsies are called upon to sing the "contrapuntal" triumphs of Egypt: Cleopatra and Catherine. In a striking image of the asp applied to the white breast of Cleopatra, Sor Juana begins with the expected ordering of sacred above secular love: "Cleopatra dies for human love: Catherine wounded by a 'better love' aspires to a 'higher' death." In a second step, however, Cleopatra's motivation for dying is transformed from that of a despairing lover to one of political resistance. She places the poisonous snake on her breast, so as not to have Augustus triumph over her "sovereign beauty." She valued her fame (honor) more than her life, and sought death through the poisonous snake rather than suffer "the prolonged death of slavery"(OC 2:167). As Cleopatra, through her death, triumphed over Augustus, in like manner Catherine, through hers, was victorious over the other tyrant, Maximus.

In the fourth poem, issues of writing, translating, and control of writing are suggested through the presentation of yet another Egyptian "triumph," the *Septuagint*. According to legend, the pre-Christian translation of Hebrew scriptures into Greek for the Hellenized Jews of Alexandria was the achievement of seventy scholars, who working independently, all arrived at the same translation. Sor Juana, however, does not emphasize the unanimity of voice of the translators and, therefore, a type of implied verbal inspiration, instead she stresses that it was Ptolemy, the pagan Egyptian king to whom the keeping of the treasures of revelation were entrusted. Further points the nun makes are: Catherine, the Egyptian, ministers to the New Covenant by translating the New Law into her "Egyptian" life and death. As Egypt (as a culture) honored the cross (the Serapis), whereas it was despised by the Romans and the Jews, so Catherine inherited in her Egyptian blood the true, though incomplete, wisdom of Egypt, and transformed its laws and cross into that of Christ. Her martyrdom on the wheel, the four quadrants of which design the cross, is imposed into the circle, sign of God, the "infinite hieroglyph," (Sor Juana's expression) which gives her life rather than death.

The sixth poem takes up the incident of Catherine and the pagan sages sent by the tyrant Maximus, whom she vanquishes with her "divine science." Here Sor Juana chooses to ignore that Catherine's effort was designed to convert the sages, and instead emphasizes the power of her mind and the "victory" of woman. "All the sages of Egypt" (origin of all wisdom) were convinced by a woman, "which proves that sex is not a factor in reasoning" (OC 2. 172). In an ironic comment on her own situation, she remarks that the real miracle was not that the men were convinced, but that they admitted it, obeying the law of reason rather than their own prejudices (OC 2:171). As true wise men, they could acknowledge the better argument. The consequence of this obedience to reason is that they are "led under the sacrificial blade," as according to legend they were put to death, which Catherine witnessed before she herself was beheaded.

The seventh poem refers to the last line in the breviary text which relates that Catherine's body was transported by angels to Mount Sinai, where it remained uncorrupted as a "vase which conserved memories of the wisdom it carried" (OC 2: 173). This is a reversal of the accepted and widely preached image of the body of woman as the "vessel of iniquity." Improving upon the Mosaic law which God wrote on stone tablets, on Catherine's beautiful body God inscribed the new law of the Gospel. Thus, not the vain pyramids on which her ancestors labored were to be her tomb, but holy Mount Sinai, where her heavenly body rested close to heaven.

LAST YEARS

THE YEARS BETWEEN the writing of the *Response* (March of 1691) and Sor Juana's death (April of 1695) have been the subject of much speculation. Did Sor Juana indeed recognize the vanity of earthly learning and withdraw into "penitential silence"? Supporters of this view include another acclaimed poet, Gabriella Mistral, the first Latin American to win the Nobel Prize for literature. Mistral sees the developments in the nun's last years as one of the "modalities of human life," such as the feverish enthusiasms of youth, the height of creative power in middle age, and the final stage being the "contrite search for the simple glass of clear water which is eternal Christian humility." [6]

Other interpreters, such as Paz, find evidence that Sor Juana was pressured into a silence that was reclusive rather than penitential, because of the coercion of church authorities such as the bishop of Puebla (Sor Philotea), the Archbishop Aguiar y Seijas, and the powerful Jesuit Núñez de Miranda. This, combined with the absence her patroness the countess of Paredes who had returned to Spain, left her isolated and in a position of unbearable vulnerability.

Several issues are central to either version. The first revolves around the interpretation of three short documents in which Sor Juana expresses her contrition and the desire to reform. Do these texts indicate that she did indeed take the bishop's admonitions to heart and withdraw from writing into a life of contemplative silence? As Paz and others have noted, nowhere in these texts does she say she has renounced writing.[7] Furthermore, I propose that since these petitions of contrition and proposed renewal of religious life are made on the anniversary of twenty-five years of her profession, they may signal a period of concentration on spiritual renewal, without necessarily carrying with them a total rejection of her intellectual life, which she had repeatedly defended as "God-given." This is all the more likely since in one of them she commits herself to a "year of scrutiny" (*aprobación*), indicating a time limit to her "withdrawal"(OC 4:521), which may have included a (temporary) self-imposed restriction on her writing and other activities. Her death in an epidemic just a month after this penitential year would have ended makes it impossible to ascertain whether she would have resumed writing as before or not. Among the effects found in her cell at her death was the poem "To the Pens of Europe" disclaiming the many encomiums (nearly one hundred pages of them) prefacing the first edition of the second volume of her works, but also revealing a keen interest in the interpretation of her writing, hardly the sign of someone who does not intend ever to publish again.

A second related question is, if she did not express a desire to stop writing, is there evidence that she was pressured to do so? The bishop's critical letter and Sor Juana's spirited response certainly imply a conflict between the nun and some church authorities. Her literary activities did go far beyond that of the ideal nun portrayed in the writings of her sometime confessor Núñez de Miranda. However, since the *Response* as well as the bishop's admonitory letter were published in 1700 in a volume intended to expand her reputation (as its title *Fame and Posthumous Works* indicates), Sor Juana's defense of her intellectual activities as a woman in the *Response* was obviously not a stance that was considered "unpublishable" or beyond the bounds of respectability, at least by a portion of the ecclesiastical establishment. Moreover, her works continued to be published during the last years of her life. The controversial *Athenagoric Letter* as well as *El Divino Narciso* were published in the first (Seville) edition of the second volume of her works in 1692, and a revised edition of this volume, without *El Divino Narciso* was published in Barcelona in 1693.

A third point of dispute is of the meaning of Sor Juana's sale of her library and scientific instruments to the Archbishop Aguiar y Seijas. Did it represent her desire to "sacrifice her intellect on the altar" as the bishop of Puebla had recommended, or was it part of a "withdrawal from the world" forced upon her by her enemies? Convent archives reveal that this sale was more complicated. The description of her first biographer, the Jesuit Calleja, does not claim she sold *all* her books to the archbishop, but only "a large quantity" of her books and worldly possessions to the archbishop to raise money for the poor. While Calleja maintains that she kept only three books and instruments of penance in her cell, convent files reveal that at Sor Juana's death Archbishop Aguiar y Seijas "in his zeal for bestowing charity, ordered that all the jewels, writings, and monies (of Sor Juana) be carried away, both those that were in the convent and those that were deposited outside it."[8] The fact that Sor Juana held back "giving up everything" may indicate that the donation of her library was made under a pressure other than spiritual.

Though it is not possible here to go beyond the sketch of the parameters of the controversy just made, or pretend to solve the enigma of her last years, I would like to point out one major element both competing "versions" have in common—both diminish Sor Juana. The first interpretation sees her as conforming unquestioningly (albeit voluntarily) to a traditionally accepted model of sanctity. The second perceives her as the victim of clerical prejudice. Neither takes sufficient account of her agency. Neither values the absolute sense of self-worth and courage which is everywhere evident in her work, even beneath formulaic expressions of self-denigration or the "rhetoric of humility." For example, in the poem "To the Pens of Europe" found in her cell at her death, though a surface theme is her astonishment at the lavish praise prefacing the second volume of her works, woven into the rather conventional frame is what amounts to a fierce assertion of her independence:

> I am not she who you think,
> but over there you have given me
> another being through your words,
> and another breath through your lips,
> and different from myself,
> I wander among your words,
> not as I am, but rather
> as you choose to imagine me.

(OC 1:159)

I suggest that Sor Juana was indeed undergoing a crisis of sorts, but that it was an intellectual rather than a spiritual one. Moreover, though signaling discouragement, it did not signal despair. To support this thesis I offer a brief analysis of one of the last texts published in her lifetime.

As we have seen, one of Sor Juana's techniques of coding is to use a short, innocuous, slightly out of place Scriptural quote which is meant to indicate to the reader a longer, more significant citation surrounding it. She uses this technique again in her dedication to Don Juan de Orue y Arbieto, the sponsor of the second volume of her work. As she establishes her common heritage with her patron, who is also a Basque, she uses among other metaphors the seemingly bland quote from Ecclesiastes "all rivers return to their sources." Through this text the nun associates herself with Ecclesiastes, who "applied his mind to know wisdom and knowledge, madness and folly" only to learn: "this is also a chase after wind. For in much wisdom there is much sorrow, and he who stores up knowledge stores up grief" (Eccl 1:17–18). She also employs two texts of the founder of her order, St. Jerome, to express her sense of intellectual isolation. Jerome had written: "No art is learned without teachers; even the dumb animals and the herd of wild creatures follow their guides" to which she comments, "but I have never known the sound of the living voice of teachers, nor have been indebted to my ears, but to my eyes for the different types of learning, having sat beneath the mute authority of books. From which seat I can say with this same saint: 'How much work I have undertaken, how many difficulties I have had to suffer, how many times I have despaired, and how many other times I have desisted and begun again, because of my determination to learn, my conscience is my witness'" (OC 4: 440–41). By using voices from the tradition—Ecclesiastes and Jerome—Sor Juana demonstrates her faithfulness to that tradition. At the same time, she claims ownership of it as a woman. She too writes of God and Wisdom in the world in spite of discouragement, like Ecclesiastes, the "Preacher."

ICONOGRAPHIC REDUCTION

HISTORICAL STUDIES OF women in all fields are revealing the degree to which the lives of women have been erased from cultural memory by neglect or antipathy. Sor Juana is unusual insofar as she was not only celebrated in her own lifetime, but is still well known as a classic literary figure in Latin America. Nonetheless, she has not escaped a second means of diminishing women's role in history when overzealous admirers reconfigure her work and the meaning of her life into a mode appropriately benign which does not challenge male hegemony. Because of the existence of five early portraits, in Sor Juana's case we are fortunate to be able to observe this dynamic at work, based not on her reception in critical articles or prefaces, but in visual form.

According to Margaret Miles' studies of the representation of women in western art, "female bodies, in the societies of the Christian West, have not represented women's subjectivity or sexuality but have, rather, been seen as a blank page on which multiple social meanings could be projected."[9] For all the admiration lavished upon her by her contemporaries in the extensive and numerous prefaces to her published works, Sor Juana's physical image did not escape the fate of being reconfigured for the male gaze. Sor Juana's own comment in verse on viewing a portrait of herself can serve as a proper caution to simplistic analysis and also as an invitation to a "disobedient reading, a reading that looks for the *effect* of the artist's or author's rhetorical or pictorial strategies rather than for the author's *intended* communication."[10]

> What you see, a colorful hoax,
> which carefully applying the beauty of art
> with the deceptive logic of color
> is a wily trick of the senses.
> This, which by flattery claims to conquer
> the rigors of time, to excuse
> the horrors of the years,
> to triumph over old age and oblivion,
> this is empty artifice,
> a fragile flower in the wind,
> a useless rein on fate,
> a foolish erring effort,
> is senile eagerness
> and, on close examination,
> is corpse, dust, shadow, void.
>
> (OC 1:277)

Of the five portraits in question, three are paintings. One by Juan de Miranda, currently in the rectory of the National Autonomous University of Mexico; one by Miguel Cabrera, in the National Historical Museum in Mexico City; one in the Philadelphia Museum of Art by an unknown artist. Two are engravings: one in the Seville edition (1692) of the second volume of her *Obras* and the other in the 1700 posthumous volume. The Miranda portrait may have been executed during Sor Juana's lifetime and completed after her death, but no later than 1714 when Miranda died. Paz's argument that it was completed in the 1680s during the period of the nun's friendship with the countess of Paredes does not take into account two elements: the panel on the writing table with biographical information gives her death date and closes with the prayer: *Requiescat in pacem.* The three volumes on the writing table bound as *Obras de la Madre Juana Inés de la Cruz* include the third volume *Fama y obras pósthumas* (Fame and Posthumous Works).[11]

The Miranda painting, which according to art historians is "reminiscent of . . . portraits of male prelates and literary figures" clearly portrays Sor Juana as an active, multifaceted personality.[12] We are apparently interrupting her as she stands at her writing pulpit. She has her quill in hand and has just signed her name under the untitled poem which begins "Green raptures" (*Verdes embellescos*). Two inkwells and letter openers frame the page on the desk. Behind them, we see three volumes with "Juana Inés de la Cruz" engraved on their spines, obviously representing her published works. The bookshelves behind her contain authors she cited and presumably loved: philosophers, theologians, poets past and contemporary. A clock, wedged among the books, peers out from the top shelf. A glass container with a plant specimen holds a paper with a geometric formula from falling off the shelf. In short we see, stylized, the "working office" of an intellectual with a wide range of interests, a writer and a poet with ink still wet on her latest creation.

Sor Juana's standing figure in its magnificent white habit of satin with long pleated sleeves and hoop skirt takes up almost half of the space of the painting. Her expression is intense, almost startled. On her chest she wears a medallion (*escudo*), part of the convent fashion of the Hieronimites and other orders of nuns in seventeenth- and eighteenth-century Latin America. "Typically depicting the Madonna, favorite saints, or a *sacra conversazione*, the *escudo* served . . . to subordinate the physiognomy of the wearer to a theological concept."[13] The painted scene on the medallion is the Annunciation, appropriate in Sor Juana's case because of her many hymns to Mary, though as one of many Marian themes, the "annunciation" itself is scarcely treated in Sor Juana's works. Here, Mary is is painted according to a tradition which portrayed her reading a book as the angel appears to her. The book was a way of representing Holy Scripture, but also of representing the Word of God which, in Mary, became flesh. For Sor Juana as a religious, there is an obvious appropriate correspondence in the image of Mary reading Holy Scripture and herself. Furthermore, one of her favorite Mariological titles "Mother of the Word" is one which, on another level, could apply to Sor Juana as a writer. In the Miranda rendering of the medallion, the book is in the center of a table, and part of the central line of the painting features a dove (the Holy Spirit) at the top, and beneath it the raised hand of the angel Gabriel as he blesses Mary. The angel and Mary are approximately the same size. Mary is not looking at the angel, but is reading. Obviously, the picture leaves open the interpretation that the angel was not a physical manifestation, but that the messenger (meaning of the original Greek *angelos*) of the revelation of God was Holy Scripture under the inspiration of the Holy Spirit.

In the 1750 painting, Cabrera obviously had the Miranda painting in mind. Sor Juana is once again in her library surrounded by numerous weighty volumes. A clock is again in evidence amidst the books. Gone are the mathematical formula and the biological specimen. She is seated rather than standing, and somewhat lost in the surrounding library, her figure occupying only about one-fourth of the area of the painting. She looks out idly at the viewer as she turns a page of an immense volume of the works of St. Jerome, the founder of her order. A small prayer book or breviary lies adjacent. Here, Sor Juana is the acceptable scholarly nun devoting herself to God and study of the "fathers," a reader rather than a writer. The quills remain in the inkwell. The inscriptions at the base of the painting are in Latin rather than in Spanish, a further signaling of the institutionalization of her image. The depiction of the Annunciation scene in the medallion echoes the themes of the larger painting. Mary is reduced to a kneeling figure less than half the size of the angel who towers over her.

Not only is there literally a reduction in stature of both female figures—Sor Juana and Mary—as the paintings move chronologically further away from her life, but there is a clearly discernable shift in the use of space within the frame, which has the effect of reducing the figure's possibilities of action outside of the gaze of the beholder. The 1750 Cabrera portrait shows Sor Juana as totally enclosed. The wall behind her is full of books. A heavy curtain drapes one corner of them. Within the space of the painting the only open space is toward the viewer. The earlier Miranda painting shows a door frame hung with a heavy brown velvet curtain on the viewer's right side. Most of the left side of Sor Juana's body is framed by the dark interior beyond the curtain frame, suggesting a space within the painting into which the figure can retreat, and also indicating that there is more to the figure than meets the eye.

Sor Juana's admiring biographer Octavio Paz's own comparison of these two portraits only reinforces the thesis of the unconsciously limiting dynamic of the male gaze. He tends to emphasize Sor Juana's body and it is difficult not to see his interpretation as the projections of male fantasy in the following excerpts:

> One hand, at once slender and rounded is white against the white sleeves of her habit and the whiteness of the paper. In Miranda's painting the hand is holding a quill pen, like a dove lifting a twig in its beak; in Cabrera's, the hand is resting on an open book, like a dove perched on a ledge. . . . Miranda's portrait shows us a rather tall woman about thirty years old. Her elegant habit falls to her feet without entirely disguising the slender waist. . . . In Cabrera's version . . . the same elegance; again the folds of the habit both emphasize and conceal the slightly parted legs and the bent right knee. In both portraits the left hand is caressing the beads of an enormous rosary worn as a necklace. The gesture is more courtly than devout. . . . The mouth is sensuous, fleshy, with just the suspicion of down on the upper lip. The nose, straight and "judicious": the flared nostrils accentuate the vague sensuality of that remote face. . . . We see Sor Juana among her books as we would glimpse naked goddesses through a break in mythological clouds, or through the foliage of a park, ladies in wide-brimmed, feathered hats.[14]

The Philadelphia portrait is the most difficult to date, with speculation ranging from its being based on a self-portrait, as the inscription beneath it claims, and possibly painted within her lifetime,[15] to the eighteenth or even early nineteenth century.[16] I am opting for a dating after the 1750 Cabrera portrait primarily because as a painting it diverges more significantly from the Miranda portrait than does Cabrera's. Here we have a half length portrait of the nun against a dark background. Outlined by the oval frame of the painting, her head and torso surrounded by darkness, give the sense of a figure suspended in a void or as painted and framed, like the scene on her medallion. In its rendering of the Annunciation scene, the medallion has Mary standing and looking at the angel rather than bent over her book. The Holy Spirit as a dove hovers over the two figures. Her face here is perhaps the most conventionally beautiful of the three. Its seriousness is softened by the trace of a smile. Missing is the background of the library with its books and traces of Sor Juana's scientific interests. She is standing next to a table, her right hand resting on the corner of a large book. Over its closed pages the painter has written: "Works of the Poetess Sor Juana Inés de la Cruz." Her left hand holds open her place in a small book (probably the breviary) which we can assume she has been reading when "interrupted." This portrait is indeed one of a beautiful nun, a poet, rather than a brilliant learned woman. She is depicted as reading rather than writing, and reading the appropriate text for her station, the breviary.

Two additional portraits, this time engravings in early editions of Sor Juana's work, reveal a similar dynamic. The first engraving is in the 1692 Seville edition of volume two of her *Obras*. Sor Juana was still alive at this time, and Paz speculates that the engraving was based on a portrait from life which the countess of Paredes, who also sponsored the volume's publication, had brought back to Spain with her.[17] The second engraving is in the 1700 first edition of *Fame and Posthumous Works*. Obviously, the *Sitz im Leben* of the engraved portraits as part of a volume of her writing is different from that of a formal portrait meant to stand alone. The engraved portraits complement, albeit in a rather superficial manner, Sor Juana's own "self-portrait" which emerges through her words. Both books contain multiple and extensive prefaces praising Sor Juana as a poet and woman of genius, aligning her with great women of the past and also contemporaries. Nonetheless, there is a similar progression of "domestication" observable between these two portraits, a progression which goes beyond that which is to be expected between the depiction of a living author and one recently deceased.

In both cases, as was customary, an elaborate iconographic frame surrounds the portrait. The 1692 frame is the simpler of the two. At the top of the page Fame, a voluptuous winged female, blows a trumpet in her left hand while holding a second trumpet aloft in her right. Sight and sound are represented in the eyes and ears which decorate her wings and reinforce the image of spreading Sor Juana's renown. Hermes, the god of medicine, but also of esoteric (hermetic) wisdom, and Athena, goddess of wisdom and of Athens (the city of the great Greek philosophers and dramatists), hold a laurel wreath above the oval frame. Their muscular arms and legs seem to be embracing the nun's portrait. The stone pedestal supporting the portrait is inscribed in Latin: "Behold a virgin in genius and piety without equal in all the world." On the oval frame of the portrait, in Spanish: "Mother Juana Inés de la Cruz. Professed nun of the convent of St. Jerome in Mexico." Beneath the pedestal a lyre, a mask, a flute, a geometer's tool, a fan, and a lute indicate Sor Juana's poetry, drama, and interest in music and scholarship.

The 1700 engraving is clearly a funerary monument. The laurel wreath which crowned her achievements in the earlier engraving, now as a funeral wreath, frames her figure. Four stone columns rise from a solid stone platform to support an arch which has as its keystone the crest of the monarchy mounted with a crown, at the center of the base also a crest with an eagle on top representing perhaps the Viceroyalty. On either side at the top of the arch two cupids recline. One holding a laurel wreath looks toward Sor Juana's figure, the other looks outward as he blows a trumpet. Here Sor Juana has been configured as a synthesis or bridge between Europe and America. On the right, in front of the columns inscribed with "America," stands the figure of an Indian—bare legged and bare chested—with bow and quiver, his hand placed tentatively over his heart as he looks down and into the distance. To the left under "Europe" a strange figure which is obviously meant to represent Spain and the conquistadors—with a plumed helmet, a shield held behind his back, and a spear in his right hand. However, since this Spaniard is smooth shaven (perhaps with a trace of a mustache) and with long flowing curls, wears a skirt and is barefooted, he makes a boyish, not to say girlish impression.

Words are more in evidence in the later engraving. The arch is inscribed with the Latin Vulgate translation of Prv 31:10: "Who can find a valiant woman? Her worth is beyond measure." Beneath the arch, but over the wreath on a ribbon-like banner the words: Hieronimite nun Sor Juana Inés de la Cruz at the age of 44 in Mexico. Beneath the wreath "Born 1651" and "Died 1695." On the stage underneath the portrait and between the columns are lute, lyre, books, a globe, a cello, the staff of Hermes. Behind the objects on the right is a mountain of ash, and on the left what appears to be a fire in the shape of a mountain. The text above and across the hills of fire and ash is the rather cryptic: "She seeks the heavens by twin hills where ashes glow and snows gleams." This is probably a reference to the place of her birth by the volcano Popocatépetl.

Another interesting contrast emerges if we consider the role of gender representation in the two engravings. In the earlier portrait, female figures predominate: Fame, Athena, and Sor Juana, plus the figure in the medallion. The 1700 version has no female figure except that of Sor Juana. Even the medallion with the figure of Mary is absent. The cupids, or cherubs, traditionally little boys, and the male figures representing America and Europe are all also curiously desexed. The allegorical figures, muscular and powerful in the earlier engraving, have become stiff and soft. Fame, the terrible yet also matronly angel in 1692 has been reconfigured into two chubby cherubs by 1700.

The most startling difference, however, of the 1692 engraving in comparison, not only with the 1700 engraving, but also with the later paintings, is the depiction of the face and costume of Sor Juana. In 1692 we see her not in formal attire with a long cape, or veil and elaborate sleeves and large medallion, but in a short veil, and a simple dress without the formal black panel. The medallion is much reduced—almost a large brooch. This time it depicts Mary Immaculate, a single woman without child, alone in the medallion, rather than the scene of the Annunciation. This is more in keeping with Sor Juana's Mariology than is the Annunciation scene. In the 1692 rendering, Sor Juana is a woman whose clothes are not principally decorative and leave her room for action. Her pen points beyond the frame surrounding her, indicating that she escapes definition by anyone other than herself, which readers of her work would have the opportunity to assess and interpret in the ensuing pages. The pen breaking the frame also suggests that what the readers will enjoy in the volume is incomplete, and that more will come from this pen in the future.

Sor Juana's figure in the funerary monument of 1700 is schematic and doll-like. She is indeed a shadow of her former self. She is in formal attire with veil, black cape, black panel, and no medallion at all. Ironically, in a fitting metaphor for the assessment of women's role in the history of culture, the quill in her hand is poised over an open book, as if making notes in the margin, suggesting that her work also is "marginal."

A final example which illustrates the temptation of later interpreters to restrict Sor Juana's voice to a manageable component, to force her into a more conventional frame, involves the erasure of her words. If we return to the Miranda portrait we notice that it contains a poem of Sor Juana's on hope, a poem, which incidentally appears only there, not in any early published volume of her works. It is also missing in the later portraits. Sor Juana would appreciate the irony of her poem on hope being "taken out of the picture" by later interpreters of her image.

I close with Sor Juana's voice as it emerges from the Miranda portrait:

> Green rapture of human life,
> crazy Hope, golden folly,
> sleep of those awake intertwined
> with dreams like vain treasures;
> soul of the world, senility luxuriant,
> decrepit youth imagined;
> the hoped for today of the happy,
> of the unhappy, the tomorrow.
> Let them follow your shadow
> in search of your light,
> those who with green panes for glasses
> see all things painted to their desire;
> and I, more measured in my fortune,
> hold in two hands my eyes,
> and see only what I touch.
>
> (OC 1:280)

Notes

Introduction

1. Others: Isabela del Campo, *Me persigue Sor Juana: juguete poético psicodramatico en once entrevistas* (México: Federación Editorial Mexicana, 1974) and Lois Hobart, *Dream of sor Juana* (El Paso, Texas, 1985). See also Frederick Luciani, "Recreaciónes de Sor Juana en la narrativa y teatro hispano/norteamericanos, 1952–88," in *Y diversa de mí misma entre vuestras plumas ando,* ed. Sara Poot Herrera (México: Colegio de México, 1993), 395–408.
2. Octavio Paz, *Sor Juana Inés de la Cruz, o las trampas de la fe* (México: Fondo de Cultura Económica, 1982).
3. Octavio Paz, *Sor Juana; or, The Traps of Faith,* trans. Margaret Sayers Peden (Cambridge, Mass: Belknap Press of Harvard University Press, 1988), 343.
4. Specifically on Sor Juana: Stephanie Merrim, "Toward a Feminist Reading of Sor Juana," in *Feminist Perspectives on Sor Juana Inés de la Cruz* (Detroit: Wayne State University Press, 1991). Includes essays by Dorothy Schons, Asunción Lavrin, Josefina Ludmer, Stephanie Merrim, Electa Arenal, Georgina Sabat-Rivers, and Ester Gimbernat De González. Stephanie Merrim, "Narciso 'desdoblado': Narcissistic Strategems in 'El Divino Narciso' and the 'Respuesta a Sor Filotea de la Cruz,'" *Bulletin of Hispanic Studies* 64, no. 2 (April 1987). Marié-Cécile Bénassy-Berling, *Humanismo y religión en Sor Juana Inés de la Cruz* (México: UNAM, 1983). Mabel Moraña, "Orden Dogmático y marginalidad en 'La Carta de Monterréy' de Sor Juana Inés de la Cruz," *Hispanic Review* 58, no. 2 (spring 1990). Kathleen A. Meyers, "Sor Juana's *Respuesta*: Rewriting the *Vitae,*" *Revista Canadiense de estudios hispánicos* 14:3 (spring 1990). Amy A. Oliver, "La ironía de 'la mas mínima criatura del mundo,'" *Cuadernos Americanos* 2, no. 1 (1988). María Esther Pérez, *Lo Americano en el teatro de Sor Juana Inés de la Cruz* (New York: Eliseo Torres and Sons, 1975). Nina Scott, "Sor Juana Inés de la Cruz: Let Your Women Keep Silence in the Churches . . . ," *Women's Studies International Forum* 8, no. 5 (1985). For studies of convent life and writings, see Electa Arenal

and Stacey Schlau, *Untold Sisters: Hispanic Nuns in Their Own Works*, trans. Amanda Powell (Albuquerque: University of New Mexico Press, 1989), which contains an excellent bibliography of primary and secondary sources; Electa Arenal, "The Convent as Catalyst for Autonomy: Two Hispanic Nuns of the Seventeenth Century," in *Women in Hispanic Literature: Icons and Fallen Idols*, ed. Beth Miller (Berkeley: University of California Press, 1983); Luis Martin, "Daughters of the Conquistadores," in *Women of the Viceroyalty of Peru* (Albuquerque: University of New Mexico, 1983); Josefina Muriel, *Cultura femenina novohispána* (México: UNAM, 1982); and Alison Weber, *Teresa of Ávila and the Rhetoric of Femininity* (Princeton: Princeton University Press, 1990).

5. Alfonso Méndez Plancarte and Alberto Salceda, eds., *Obras Completas de Sor Juana Inés de la Cruz*, vol. 1–4 (México-Buenos Aires: Fondo de Cultura Económica, 1951–57). All citations of Sor Juana's works from Méndez Plancarte and Salceda's edition will be inserted in the text using the abbreviation OC, for *Obras Completas*, followed by the volume: page number.line.

6. Jean Franco, "Sor Juana Explores Space," in *Plotting Women: Gender and Representation in Mexico* (New York: Columbia University Press, 1989).

7. Ibid., 23.

8. Sara Poot Herrera, ed., *Υ diversa de mí misma entre vuestras plumas ando* (México: El Colegio de México, 1993).

9. Alan S. Trueblood, trans., *A Sor Juana Anthology* (Cambridge, Mass.: Harvard University Press, 1988); Margaret Sayers Peden, trans., *A Woman of Genius: The Intellectual Autobiography of Sor Juana Inés de la Cruz* (Salisbury, Conn.: Lime Rock Press, Inc., 1982); Electa Arenal and Amanda Powell, trans., *The Answer/La Respuesta: Including a Selection of Poems* (New York: The Feminist Press at the City University of New York, 1994).

10. As a result I will also not be considering Sor Juana's philosophical poem, *First Dream*.

1: POINTS OF DEPARTURE

1. Paz, Sayers Peden, trans., *Sor Juana*, 66. Unless otherwise indicated, all translations of Sor Juana's works are my own.

2. I am citing the text of Calleja's biography as in Herón Pérez Martínez, *Estudios Sorjuanianos* (Morelia, Michoacán: Instituto Michoacano de Cultura, 1988), 132.

3. OC 1:lviii.

4. Paz, *Sor Juana*, 65. Editor Méndez Plancarte speculates that Sor Juana is Calleja's source for the date of her birth, and he sees the

nun's feminine vanity taking years off her age. He remarks: "Even St. Teresa, though a saint, took two years off her age . . . !" In Sor Juana's *Inundación Castálida* (Madrid: Clásicos Castalia, 1983), 15, editor Georgina Sabat de Rivers, reacting to Méndez Plancarte, protests that to accept the earlier date would "deny the truth of what Sor Juana says in the *Response*" and would call into question whether she were really a child prodigy. By Sor Juana's own account she "had not yet celebrated her third birthday" when she began to learn to read, but she does not give a date of birth.

5. Pérez Martínez, *Estudios Sorjuanianos,* 132.
6. Guillermo Ramírez España, *La familia de Sor Juana Inés de la Cruz. Documentos inéditos* (México: Imprenta Universitaria, 1947), 17. An even earlier official documentation of Isabel Ramírez's "natural" children is the will of Pedro Ramírez, her father, who in 1655 (or 1659), after listing his 11 children, listed again, separately, those who married with their spouses.
7. OC 1:xxvii.
8. Colin M. MacLachlan and Jaime E. Rodríguez O., *The Forging of the Cosmic Race: A Reinterpretation of Colonial Mexico* (Berkeley: University of California Press, 1980), 229, write of the general "acceptance of extramarital arrangements, often on a permanent basis."
9. Paz, *Sor Juana,* 70.
10. Dorothy Schons, "Some Obscure Points in the Life of Sor Juana Inés de la Cruz," in Merrim, *Feminist Perspectives,* 42.
11. Sabat de Rivers, *Inundación,* 15.
12. Paz, trans. Sayers Peden, *Sor Juana,* 66.
13. Ibid.
14. Probably Sor Juana had heard of Catalina de Erauso. This extraordinary woman had escaped from a convent in Spain to flee to America in men's clothes. For years she was able to hide her feminine identity as she fought against the Indians, operated in the underworld in Peru and Chile, and was finally feted in Europe, even by the pope, when her subterfuge was discovered. She spent the last years of her life still in men's clothing as a mule driver between Vera Cruz and Mexico City.
15. Paz, *Sor Juana,* 78.
16. Pérez Martínez, *Estudios Sorjuanianos,* 135.
17. Paz, *Sor Juana,* 86.
18. Pérez Martínez, *Estudios Sorjuanianos,* 134.
19. Ibid., 136.
20. Irving Leonard, *Baroque Times in Old Mexico* (Ann Arbor: University of Michigan Press, 1959), 130–44, describes several poetry tournaments held in seventeenth-century Mexico.

21. Pérez Martínez, *Estudios Sorjuanianos,* 137.
22. Antonio Alatorre, "La Carta de Sor Juana al P. Núñez," *Nueva Revista de Filología Hispánica* 35 (1987): 661–62.
23. Moraña, "Orden Dogmático," 216–17.
24. This statement, together with Sor Juana's friendship with the next vicereine, María Luisa Manrique de Lara y Gonzaga, Countess of Paredes (1680–88), and her poems celebrating this friendship, have been the source her of characterization in plays and film as a lesbian, a characterization most scholars find impossible to ascertain, given a wide range of acceptable expression of women's friendships and the stylized poetic rendering of Sor Juana's passionate declarations to the countess of Paredes, the "Lysis" of her poems.
25. Bénassy-Berling, *Humanismo,* 452.
26. Alatorre, "Carta," 623–24.
27. Ibid., 660.
28. Sabat de Rivers, *Inundación,* 15.
29. Considering the extent to which Sor Juana's relationship with prominent churchmen in her life have been the subject of intense analysis, it is strange that Enríquez de Rivera, who was archbishop of Mexico City from 1668 to 1682 and viceroy from 1673 to 1680, has been neglected. He is not mentioned by Calleja, and Paz devotes a comparatively limited space to him. This, in spite of his having been Sor Juana's ultimate ecclesiastical superior for 13 years, from the time she entered the convent until she was in her early thirties.
30. Hubert H. Bancroft, *History of Mexico,* vol. 3: 1600–1803. Vol. 11 of *The Works of Hubert Howe Bancroft* (San Francisco: The History Company Publishers, 1887), 182.
31. Paz, *Sor Juana,* 138.
32. Bancroft, *The Works,* 11:182–83.
33. Spanish playwrights Tirso de Molina and Anastasio Pantaleón de Rivera, Mexican poet Fray Miguel de Guevara, and the young dramatist Salazar y Torres who had grown up in Mexico.
34. Paz, *Sor Juana,* 133–34.

2. GOD AMONG THE NATIONS

1. Carlos de Sigüenza y Góngora, "Teatro de virtudes políticas," in *Obras Históricas,* ed. Jose Rajas Garcidueñas (México: Editorial Porrúa, 1960), 246.
2. Ibid., 238–39.
3. Ibid., 230.
4. Lewis Hanke, *Aristotle and the American Indians: A Study in Race*

Prejudice in the Modern World (Chicago: Henry Regnery Company 1959), 97.

5. Bénassy-Berling, *Humanismo*, 308, 312.
6. Benjamin Keen, *The Aztec Image in Western Thought* (New Brunswick, N.J.: Rutgers University Press, 1985), 118–21.
7. Georgina Sabat de Rivers summarizes the origin and place of such ceremonies as well as their political import in her article, "El Neptuno de Sor Juana: Fiesta barroca y programa politíco," in *University of Dayton Review* 16, no. 2 (1983): 63–65.
8. OC 4:378; Sigüenza y Góngora, "Teatro," 232.
9. Sigüenza y Góngora, "Teatro," 234.
10. Electa Arenal, "Where Woman is Creator of the Wor(l)d. Or, Sor Juana's Discourses on Method," in Merrim, *Feminist Perspectives*, 130–31.
11. Sabat de Rivers, "El Neptuno," 68.
12. "Cicero, Marcus Tullius," *The New Encyclopedia Britannica* (Chicago: Encyclopedia Britannica, 1986), 3:314.
13. See also: Salceda, OC 4:xxxiix; and Sabat de Rivers, "El Neptuno," 63–73.
14. Sigüenza y Góngora, "Teatro," 244.
15. Ibid., 245.
16. Paz, *Sor Juana*, 450–51.
17. Alatorre, "Carta," 513.
18. Ibid., 616–17 cites the most important of these.
19. Paz, trans. Sayers Peden, *Sor Juana*, 496–97.
20. Ibid., 497.
21. Moraña, "Orden Dogmático," 211.
22. Paz, *Sor Juana*, 500.
23. Ibid., 501.
24. Ibid., 500.
25. Ibid., 502.
26. Ibid., 500.
27. Alatorre, "Carta," 666–67.

3: COMEDIES TO THE HONOR AND GLORY OF BREAD

1. Cited by Méndez Plancarte from *El Nombre de Jesús* of Lope de Vega, OC 3:lix.
2. Ibid., lix.
3. Ibid., 3:lvi.
4. Calvin and Zwingli emphasized a symbolic presence, Luther saw it only as "real presence" during the celebration of the community in the Mass.

5. In Calderón's *auto El Sacro Parnaso* "Porque dijo un gran sujeto / que el día de Corpus era / contra el hereje argumento, el cascabel de un danzante: / quierendo decir, con esto que en el gran día de Dios, / quien no está loco, no es cuerdo"(OC 3:lx). And in another of his *loas El Árbol del Mejor Fruto*: "era cada cascabel de un danzante, silogismo / contra el apóstata infiel" (OC 3:lix).

6. The Catechism of the Council of Trent for pastors, which provided a basic summary of religious teachings for priests, devotes thirteen pages to the real presence and transubsantiation out of the forty-three in the chapter devoted to the Eucharist.

7. Gregory the Great, *Dialogues*, 3.31.

8. OC 3:lxxix.

9. W. Goffart, "Hermenegild, St.," in *New Catholic Encyclopedia*, vol. 6. (Washington, D.C.: Catholic University Press, 1967), 1074–75.

10. Alberto Arturo García Carraffa, *Enciclopedia heráldica y genealógica hispano-americana* (Madrid: Impro. de A Marzo, 1919), 48: 167.

11. He also wonders how the official censors could have overlooked this inaccuracy.

12. OC 3:lv.

13. We find Sor Juana using the same references in her critique of Vieira's sermon.

14. Saint Thomas Aquinas, *Summa Theologiciae*, 3a.79,I. "O Sacrament of piety, O sign of unity, O bond of charity, o vinculum caritatis!"

15. Ramón A. Gutiérrez, *When Jesus Came, the Corn Mothers Went Away: Marriage, Sexuality, and Power in New Mexico, 1500–1846* (Stanford, Calif.: Stanford University Press, 1991), 137–40.

16. OC 3:599.

17. OC 3:603–6.

18. The obvious contradiction between the proclaimed intent of the *auto* to catechize the ignorant Indians and the Christian background necessary to read the story of Joseph as a pre-figuring of eucharistic truths only underscores that the intended recipients of the combined message of *loa* and *auto* is an audience representing the Christian conquerors.

19. Though the strong emphasis on faith is a major part of the Epistle to the Hebrews and, as it is in this letter that we find the reference to the tip of Joseph's scepter, given the question taken up in the *loa,* i.e., the Indians' continuing high estimation of (human) sacrifice as a means of showing highest devotion to God, it is odd that she does not refer also to chapters nine and ten of this same letter, which make the argument that Christ's shedding of his own blood "once for all" made other sacrifices redundant.

20. Most scholars consider the God in question to be Huizilopochtli (OC 3:504). Early in the conquest of Mexico, Pedro de Alvarado

"ordered an unprovoked massacre of the leading Aztec chiefs and warriors as they celebrated with song and dance a high religious festival in honor of Huizilopochtli." See Keen, *Aztec Image*, 54.

21. In the disputations of 1550, Sepúlveda argued that, because in the Old Testament God destroyed idolatrous peoples, it was justifiable to wage war on the Indians, destroying their religious culture even before they were missionized. *Tratados de Fray Bartolomé de Las Casas*, ed. Lewis Hanke, et al. (México: Fondo de Cultura Económica, 1965), 1:337.

22. Sometimes the Indians regarded the missionaries as demented because of their strange language and ascetic practices. Juan Guillermo Durán, *Monumenta Catechetica Hispanoamericana* (Buenos Aires: Facultad de Teologia de la Pontifica Universidad, 1986), 1:90–94.

23. Similarly, only after it became apparent that the Indians were not easily converted by mere exhortation did the missionaries begin to ask them questions about their religion and culture, initiating what were to become the great studies of Sahagún, Motolinía, Durán, and others.

24. Lewis Hanke, *All Mankind Is One: A Study of the Disputation between Bartolomé de Las Casas and Juan Ginés de Sepúlveda in 1550 on the Intellectual and Religious Capacity of the American Indians* (Dekalb, Ill.: Northern Illinois University Press, 1974), 93–94. Chapter 35 refers to *Defense*. Also, Gustavo Gutiérrez, *Las Casas in Search of the Poor of Jesus Christ*, trans. Robert Barr (Maryknoll, N.Y.: Orbis, 1993), 178–81.

25. All quotes from *El Divino Narciso* are my translation of the verses cited in OC 3:3–97.

26. The similarity of the two feasts had long been noted. See Augustín de Vetancurt, *Teatro Mexicano: Descripción breve de los sucessos exemplares de la Nueva-España en el nuevo mundo occidental de las Indias* (Madrid: Jose Porrúa Turanzas, 1960), 415.

4: MARY AS DIVINE (M)OTHER

1. Jeanette Rodríguez, *Our Lady of Guadalupe: Faith and Empowerment among Mexican-American Women* (Austin: University of Texas Press, 1994), 17.

2. Ibid., 38.

3. Ibid., 37.

4. Ibid., 8.

5. Ibid., 30.

6. Alan R. Sandstrom, "The Tonantsi Cult of the Eastern Nahua," in *Mother Worship: Theme and Variations*, ed. James Preston (Chapel

Hill: University of North Carolina Press, 1982), 11:25–50, reports that even in contemporary Nahuatl villages: "one female deity is the most important member of the Nahua pantheon. This is the goddess Tonantsi, whose name can be translated from Nahuatl as 'our sacred mother,'" 26. See reference in Ena Campbell's "The Virgin of Guadalupe and the Female Self-Image: A Mexican Case History," also in the same volume, 5–24.

7. Rodriguez, *Lady of Guadalupe*, 45–46.

8. See, also, OC 2:139 for a similar image.

9. Rafael Catalá, *Para una lectura Americana del barroco Mexicano: Sor Juana Inés de la Cruz y Sigüenza y Góngora* (Minneapolis: The Prisma Institute, 1987), 117–21.

10. George Tavard, *Juana Inés de la Cruz and the Theology of Beauty: The First Mexican Theology* (Notre Dame, Ind.: University of Notre Dame Press, 1991), 96–97. Sor Juana frequently refers to the woman in Revelation for the feasts of the Conception of Mary and her Assumption into Heaven, references which would have been suggested by the liturgical readings for these feasts. Examples: OC: 2:226, 227, 239, 257.

11. Tavard, *Theology of Beauty*, 98.

12. E.Thomas Stanford, "Villancico, Latin America," *The New Grove Dictionary of Music and Musicians*, ed. Stanley Sadie, 19 vols. (London: Macmillan, 1980), 19: 769–70.

13. Barbara Babcock discusses aspects of the relationship of humor and ritual. Barbara A. Babcock, "Arrange Me into Disorder: Fragments and Reflections on Ritual Clowning," in *Rite, Drama, Festival, Spectacle*, ed. John J. MacAloon (Philadelphia: Institute for the Study of Human Issues, 1984), 102–28.

14. Barbara Myerhoff gives a concise summary of the "work of ritual." Barbara G. Myerhoff, "A Death in Due Time: Construction of Self and Culture in Ritual Drama," in MacAloon, *Rite, Drama*, 151f.

15. I am reminded of Thérèse of Lisieux's plaintive lines: "Praying the rosary is more painful for me than wearing a hairshirt." *Manuscrits autobiographiques* (Paris: Carmel de Lisieux, 1957), 190–91.

16. Donald Weinstein and Rudolph Bell, *Saints and Society: The Two Worlds of Western Christendom, 1000–1700* (Chicago: University of Chicago Press, 1982).

17. Caroline Walker Bynum, *Holy Feast and Holy Fast* (Berkeley: University of California Press, 1987), 318. Bynum also reports Simone Roisin's findings that in visions of Cistercians in thirteenth-century northern Europe, the virgin seemed more important to men, the humanity of Christ to women. Simone Roisin, *L'Hagiographie cistercienne dans le diocèse de Liège au XIIIe siècle* (Louvain: Bibliothèque de l'Université, 1947), 108, 111–20.

18. Lumen Gentium 8 par 67.
19. Bénassy-Berling, *Humanismo*, 236.
20. Tavard, *Theology of Beauty*, 99.
21. Elizabeth A. Johnson, "Mary and the Female Face of God," *Theological Studies* 50 (1989): 504.
22. Ibid., 501.
23. OC 2:462.
24. OC 2:414.
25. Though Bénassy-Berling, *Humanismo*, 252, sees the *Exercicios* as having a markedly Christological, as opposed to Marian accent, and moving away from emphasis on Mary; given its structuring motif, Mary's presence at the creation, and the fact that the feast of the Annunciation is here called "Incarnation," I consider it essentially Marian.
26. Tavard, *Theology of Beauty*, 90–94.
27. Ignatius Loyola, *The Spiritual Exercises of St. Ignatius Loyola*, trans. Lewis Delmage (Boston, Mass.: Daughters of St. Paul, 1978), 25–27.
28. María de Ágreda, *The Conception*, vol. 2 of *City of God: The Divine History and Life of the Virgin Mother of God*, trans. Marison Fiscar (New York: Alfred A. Knopf, 1976), 28.9.
29. Ibid., 29.10.
30. In the laurentian litany one of Mary's titles is "Mystical Rose" (OC 4:482–83).
31. Sor Juana's oblique reference to the vow honoring the doctrine of the Immaculate Conception, "to the point of being prepared to shed blood in its defense," may be interpreted as an indication of how common this practice was. On the other hand, she apparently waited many years, until March of 1694, to make such a vow herself, in spite of her obvious devotion to this particular Marian doctrine.

5: BOLD ADVENTURESS: MARY AS A MODEL FOR WOMEN

1. Bernard of Clairvaux, *Magnificat: Homilies in Praise of the Blessed Virgin Mary*, trans. Maríe-Bernard Said and Graci Perigo (Kalamazoo, Mich.: Cistercian Publications, 1979), 34.
2. Ibid., 12.
3. Ibid., 9.
4. Ágreda, *City of God*, 2:31.15.
5. Pope John Paul II, *The Mother of the Redeemer: Redemptoris Mater* (Washington, DC: United States Catholic Conference, 1987), 37.18.
6. Marina Warner, *Alone of All Her Sex: The Myth and the Cult of the Virgin Mary* (New York: Alfred A. Knopf, 1976).

7. Nicholas Perry and Loreto Echeverría, *Under the Heel of Mary* (London: Routledge, 1988).
8. Elizabeth A. Johnson, "The Marian Tradition and the Reality of Women," *Horizons* 12, no. 1 (1985): 117.
9. OC 2:425.
10. H. Diane Russell and Bernadine Barnes, *Eva/Ave: Woman in Renaissance and Baroque Prints* (Washington, D.C.: National Gallery of Art and The Feminist Press at CUNY, 1990).
11. OC 2:25: "Without the stain of Adam's fault she was conceived." OC 2:21: "She alone was freed from the taint of Adam." OC 2:88: "She is not daughter of Adam, she is mother of God." Also, OC 2:103.
12. OC 2:363–64 translates the poem into modern Spanish.
13. OC 2:16 in a reference to Song of Songs 1:5.
14. OC 2:364–65 gives background on the dance as well as a prose and verse translation into Spanish from the Nahuatl.
15. Translations from OC 2:365.
16. For an in depth analysis of the relationship of women's bodies to religious imagery, also see Bynum, *Holy Feast*.
17. Johnson, "Marian Tradition," 132.
18. Ibid.
19. Tavard, *Theology of Beauty*, 40.
20. In the Spanish church, an illegitimate child was called a daughter or son "of the church" on their baptismal certificate. Given Sor Juana's own background, this reference undoubtedly has personal resonance, especially because, as an adjective, the type *bastarda* is feminine, so that the grammatically feminine *letra* becomes *hija de la iglesia*, the exact wording on the nun's own baptismal certificate.

6: On the Benefits of Christ's Love: Athenagoric letter

1. Constance M. Montross, *Virtue or Vice? Sor Juana's Use of Thomistic Thought* (Lanham, Md.: University Press of America, 1982), 20.
2. Franco, "Sor Juana Explores," 38.
3. W. Frasier Mitchell, *English Pulpit Oratory from Andrewes to Tillotson* (London: SPCK, 1932), 3–4.
4. C.R. Boxer, *A Great Luso-Brazilian figure: Padre António Vieira, S.J., 1608–1697* (London: Hispanic and Luso-Brazilian Councils, 1957), 4.
5. Robert Ricard, "António Vieira et Sor Juana Inés de la Cruz," *Bulletin des Études Portugaises et de l'Institut Français au Portugal* 12 (1948): 1.
6. Paz, *Sor Juana*, 524. On the possible translations available to Sor Juana see Ricard, "António Vieira," 20–21.

7. Matthias C. Kiemen, *The Indian Policy of Portugal in the Amazon Region, 1614–1693* (New York: Farrar, Straus and Giroux, 1973), 79.

8. Antonio Alatorre, "Para Leer *La Fama y Obras Pósthumas* de Sor Juana Inés de la Cruz," *Nueva Revista de Filología Hispánica* 29, no. 2 (1980): 449. Boxer, *Padre Antonio Vieira*, 3.

9. Fauchón Royer's biography of Sor Juana, *The Tenth Muse* (Patterson, N.J.: St. Anthony Guild Press, 1952), contains the only English translation of the *Letter*.

10. Paz, *Sor Juana*, 392–93. Almost without exception, contemporary scholars consider Sor Juana's *Letter* a most tedious work, an overly subtle commentary of Vieira's already labored and obscure theme of the *finezas* of Christ. Robert Ricard calls it "more curious than admirable" and warns the reader that his own summary of it will be excessively subtle and ponderous. Ricard, "António Vieira," 4.

11. Paz, *Sor Juana*, 433.

12. Vieira, OC 4:674. A point very like Sor Juana's above, in which the suffering of the presence of insults is greater than the suffering of absence.

13. Vieira, OC 4:677.

14. Ibid., 4:680–81.

15. Tavard, *Theology of Beauty*, 145, indicates as much.

16. The original 1689 *Letter* cites Bible chapter and verse in the margins, and the 1692 edition of *Letter* included at least one patristic reference to a sermon of Gregory, the quote of which appears to have been taken from the Roman breviary ordinary of a pope confessor (OC 4:645). In *Response,* she cites patristic and contemporary sources.

17. Ricard, "António Vieira," 29–34.

18. Vieira, OC 4:689.

19. Ibid., 4:685.

20. Ibid., 4:688–89.

21. Ibid., 4:689. For further discussion, see Paz, *Sor Juana*, 390.

22. Montross, *Virtue or Vice?*, 9.

23. Whether this is because she was working with a defective translation or for some hidden reason of her own is not clear. Ricard, "António Vieira," 9, mentions this possibility.

24. Vieira, OC 4:690.

25. What some might see as emerging rationalism, others see as appropriation of the scholastic dialectic. Montross, *Virtue or Vice?*, 17, maintains: "Scholastic and Aristotelian philosophy, logic, rhetoric, and terminology provide the intellectual framework for the letter."

26. "Vieira's basic rhetorical and logical technique is syllogistic reasoning." Montross, *Virtue or Vice?*, 3–5.
27. OC 4:687. Vieira's own political involvement was so intense and varied that generalizations are impossible. Strangest of all, for me, were his millenistic ideas, which are nowhere evident in the *manda-to* sermon Sor Juana critiqued, but which appear to have been a powerful motivating force for this extremely complex man. Raymond Cantel, *Prophétisme et messiansisme dans l'oeuvre d'António Vieira* (Paris: Ediciones Hispano-Americanas, 1960).
28. Vieira, OC 4:692.

7: THE NUN AND THE BISHOP: DRAMA OF POWER

1. Franco, "Sor Juana Explores," 39.
2. Elbert N.S. Thompson, *Literary Bypaths of the Renaissance* (New Haven: Yale University Press, 1924), 91.
3. Ibid., 91–92.
4. Ibid., 95–100.
5. Bénassy-Berling, *Humanismo*, 166–70, disputes that the *Letter* and the subsequent letters were the result of a crisis. She also maintains, with the editors of the critical edition of Sor Juana's work, Méndez Plancarte and A.G. Salceda, that the addressee is never identified and remains unknown. It is not clear, however, what proof Salceda has that the *Letter* passed from one hand to the other, finally arriving in the hands of the bishop of Puebla, Manuel Fernández de Santa Cruz (OC 4:xxxix), rather than being directly sent to him. Paz, *Sor Juana*, 520, Franco, "Sor Juana Explores," 41, Tavard, *Theology of Beauty*, 135, Muriel, *Cultura femenina*, 226 support the theory that the person soliciting the *Letter* and prefacing its publication under the pseudonym Sor Philotea de la Cruz was the bishop of Puebla.
6. Paz, *Sor Juana*, 520–22.
7. Franco, "Sor Juana Explores," 22–31.
8. Ibid., 25.
9. See Curtius on distinction and interconnection of "submission formula" and "protestation of incapacity". Ernst Robert Curtius, *European Literature and the Latin Middle Ages*, trans. Willard R. Trask (New York: Pantheon Books, 1953), 410–13.
10. Weber, *Teresa of Ávila*, 51.
11. Ibid., 42–76 explores in detail what she terms the rhetoric of humility in chapter two of her study.
12. Scott, "Silence in the Churches," 514.
13. Ibid.

14. Weber, *Teresa of Ávila*, 50.

15. Ibid.

16. Emphasis mine.

17. Paz, *Sor Juana*, 391 comments "very well hidden."

18. Ibid., 481.

19. Miguel de Cervantes, *Don Quixote*, trans., John Ormsby, ed. Joseph Jones and Kenneth Douglas (New York/London: W.W. Norton, 1980), 9.

20. OC 4:434. Paul Julian Smith, *Writing in the Margin. Spanish Literature of the Golden Age* (Oxford: Clarendon Press, 1988), 18.

21. Oliver, "La Ironía," 64–71.

22. Montross, *Virtue or Vice?*, 18.

23. Bénassy-Berling, *Humanismo*, 166.

24. Franco, "Sor Juana Explores," 43.

25. Josefina Ludmer, "Tretas del débil," in *La sartén por el mango*, ed. Patricia Elena González and Eliana Ortega (Rio Piedras, P.R.: Ediciones EB Huracán, 1985), 51.

26. Peter N. Skrine, *The Baroque: Literature and Culture in Seventeenth-Century Europe* (New York: Holmes & Meier Publishers, 1978), 1–25.

27. Ludmer, "Tretas del débil," 51.

28. Francis de Sales, *Introduction to the Devout Life*, trans. John K. Ryan (New York: Longmans, 1962), xxvii. French: François de Sales, *Introduction à la vie dévote* (Paris: Editions du Seuil, 1962), 13.

29. Alatorre, "Para leer," 498. Franco, "Sor Juana Explores," 43.

30. Schons, "Obscure Points," 59

31. Angelo Morino, "Respuesta a sor Juana Inés," *Cuadernos Hispano-Americanos* 450 (Dec. 1987): 7–36.

32. OC 4:696

33. Montross, *Virtue or Vice?*, 18.

34. OC 4:695–96.

35. Recently (1988), Patricio Lizama, "Sor Filotea y Sor Juana: la conversión y la denuncia," *Discurso literario* 6.1 (1988): 203–17, again made a case for the interaction of nun and bishop in terms of conversion. Santa Cruz calls Sor Juana to a conversion which summons her to a new form of life, a new relationship with God, which in *Response* she rejects.

36. Lizama, "Sor Filotea," 207.

37. Paz, *Sor Juana*, 402–3.

38. Ibid., 410.

39. Bénassy-Berling, "Más sobre la conversión de Sor Juana," *Nueva Revista de Filología Hispánica* 32, no. 2 (1983): 462–71; Ricard,

"Antonio Vieira," 11–13; Tavard, *Theology of Beauty*, 167–68; Franco, "Sor Juana Explores," 42–43.

40. Paz, *Sor Juana*, 5. Emphasis mine.
41. Ibid., 412.
42. Bénassy-Berling, "Más," 464.
43. Ibid., 465.
44. Paz, *Sor Juana*, 412.
45. Ibid., 409–10.
46. Oliver, "La Ironía," 64–71.
47. Scott, "Silence in the Church," 511–19. Electa Arenal, "The Convent," 164–83.
48. Rosa Perelmuter-Pérez, "La estructura retórica de la *Respuesta a Sor Filotea*," *Hispanic Review* 51, no. 2 (1983): 147–58.
49. Merrim, "Feminist Reading," 11–37; Merrim, "Narciso," 111–17; Ludmer, "Tretas del debil," 47–54; Moraña, "Orden Dogmático," 205–25; Franco, "Sor Juana Explores," 23–54.
50. Méndez Plancarte, OC 4:xlii–xliii.
51. Ibid., OC 4:435.42–44. For a discussion of dimensions of irony in the *Response* see Oliver, "La Ironía," 64–71.
52. Moraña, "Orden Dogmático," 216.
53. To Franco, "Sor Juana Explores," 44: "The transparent fiction of the pseudonym 'Sor Filotea' is turned into a double-edged weapon, permitting an exaggerated deference to the recipient who is supposed to be a powerless woman and, thus, exposing the real power relations behind the egalitarian mask."
54. Leonard, *Baroque Times*, 117–23.
55. Though also unusual for a man to adopt a feminine pseudonym, as bishop Santa Cruz does, he was not unique in doing so. Even a study as limited in scope as Ricard's study of the reception of the *Letter* led him to discover two other instances. Another, which appeared in Lisbon in 1727, entitled *Apologia a favor do R.P. Antonio Vieyra* was ostensibly by Sor Margarida Ignacián, but in reality by her brother, Luis Gonçalves Pinheiro. In a second instance, the editor of a collection of Vieira's works who included the *Athenagoric Letter* assumes that "Sor Juana" was the pseudonym of a certain P.M. Guerra. Ricard's comment: "Thus the whole incident assumed the characteristics of a masked ball," is indicative of the spirit in which Sor Juana forges her literary game with the bishop, a spirit her contemporaries obviously shared. Ricard, "António Vieira," 16,25.
56. Perelmuter Pérez, "La estructura retórica," 147–58, an enlightening analysis of classical rhetorical and forensic patterns.
57. According to legend, Thomas sat for years in Albertus Magnus's classes never speaking a word, which won for him the nickname, "the dumb ox."

58. Sharon Larisch, "Sor Juana's *Apologia*," *Pacific Coast Philology* 21, no. 1–2 (Nov., 1986): 49.
59. Ibid., 52; Arenal, "The Convent," 178.

8: FOLLOWING JESUS: CONFESSION, CONVERSION, APOLOGIA

1. Franco, "Sor Juana Explores," 45–47.
2. Lizama, "Sor Filotea," 214.
3. Larisch, "Sor Juana's *Apologia*," 48: "Thus Socrates reveals the existence of his private voice as part of his apology published by Plato; St. Paul testily recounts his life in the face of public distrust; Cardinal Newman discloses his conscience and conversion in order to refute charges made against him by Protestant clergymen and the novelist Charles Kingsley."
4. Ibid., 52.
5. Paz, *Sor Juana*, 499.
6. Meyers, "Rewriting the *Vitae*,"460.
7. *The Confessions of St. Augustine*, trans. F.J. Sheed (New York: Sheed & Ward, 1965), 12–13.
8. Ibid., 22.
9. Trueblood, trans. *Sor Juana Anthology*, 211.
10. *Confessions*, 41.
11. Ibid.
12. Ibid., 17–18.
13. Ibid., 22.
14. Paz, *Sor Juana*, 109.
15. Marc Antonio Loera de la Llave, " . . . Sirtes tocando/de imposibiles . . . en Sor Juana Inés de la Cruz," *Cuadernos Americanos* 265, no. 2 (Mar.–Apr., 1986): 133.
16. Trueblood, trans. *Sor Juana Anthology*, 209. Sayers Peden, trans. *Woman of Genius*, 24.
17. "Sor Juana, like Socrates, the father of Western Philosophy, cannot, because of her deep respect for wisdom, claim to be wise. Indeed, she is a lover of wisdom, but not its possessor." Luis Cortest, "Some Thoughts on the Philosophy of Sor Juana Inés de la Cruz," *Inti* 21 (spring 1985): 86.
18. Oliver, "La Ironía," 69.
19. Plato, *Five Dialogues*, trans. G.M.A. Grube, (Indianapolis Ind: Hackett Publishing Co., 1981), 26.
20. Ibid., 34.
21. Trueblood, trans. *Sor Juana Anthology*, 223.
22. Cortest, "Some Thoughts," 88.
23. Even today there is a "St. Socrates Society" in the U.S. whose members are primarily teachers of literature and philosophy.

24. Lines 183–84 of the *Letter of Monterréy*, in Alatorre, "*Carta*," 623. Paz, trans. Sayers Peden, *Sor Juana*, 499.
25. Elaine Showalter, "Feminist Criticism in the Wilderness," in *The New Feminist Criticism: Essays on Women, Literature, and Theory*, ed. Showalter (New York: Pantheon, 1985), 264.
26. Thomas à Kempis, *The Imitation of Christ*, trans. W. Creasy (Macon, Ga.: Mercer University Press, 1989), 48–51.
27. Franco, "Sor Juana Explores," 43.
28. Ludwig Pfandl, *Juana Inés de la Cruz, die zehnte Muse von Mexico: Ihr Leben, ihre Dichtung ihre Psyche* (Munich: H. Rinn, 1946).
29. She connects "the narcissistic posturing of Sor Juana's autobiographical *yo*" in the *Response* and *El Divino Narciso* "as verbal figuration, as *con*figuration of the work and, finally as *pre*figuration of the *yo* of the *Response*." Merrim, "Narciso," 111.
30. Teresa de Ávila, *Obras de Santa Teresa de Jesús* (Madrid: Editorial Apostolado de la Prensa, 1964), 1120.
31. "Cántico Espiritual," in *Obras de San Juan de la Cruz* (Madrid: Editorial Apostolado de la Prensa, 1966), 553.
32. OC 4:695.
33. Teresa of Ávila, *Obras*, 541.
34. Ibid., 656, 654–55.
35. Ibid., 652, 654.
36. "Woman, I do not know what you are saying" (Lk. 22:60) and "Woman, I do not know him"(Lk 22:57). This second quote is a variation on the actual text which has Jesus talking to a man, and may be seen as part of the game of disguise the nun is playing with the bishop.
37. That famous fool of Spanish literature Don Quixote was also obsessed with books and with romances. He, too, was sick at one time and his friends hid his books from him.
38. Blaise Pascal, *Oeuvres Complètes*, ed. Jacques Chevalier (France: Editions Gallimard, 1954), 4.
39. Ibid., 2–7, 57–70.

9: IN COUNTLESS NUMBERS: THE TRADITION OF LEARNED WOMEN

1. Catholic doctrine, based on Rom 1:19–32 and Rom 8:19–25, considers God's revelation to be in nature as well as in Scripture.
2. Montross, *Virtue or Vice?*, 27 writes: "The world became her book when she was forbidden to study. Most importantly, what and how she learned outside of books corresponded to the methods, aims and content of the liberal arts. Sor Juana, in this way, justifies her learning and that of all women by fitting it into the

mold of traditional learning. The world is seen as a harmonious machine in which all the parts worked together and which led her to a knowledge of God."

3. In other contexts as, Curtius points out, the same interrelatedness of disciplines was used to justify poetry as the highest form of knowing in late Renaissance literary circles, including Lope de Vega. Ernst Robert Curtius, "Theological Art-theory in Spanish Literature," in *European Literature and the Latin Middle Ages*, trans. Willard R. Trask (New York: Pantheon Books, 1953), 548–50.

4. Trueblood translates this "padres" as "fathers."

5. Paz, *Sor Juana*, 408.

6. Bénassy, in her article "Más sobre la conversión de Sor Juana," makes the point that although Aguiar y Seijas has these things said of him, there is no record of his having refused to confirm women, for example. Though the above description is exaggerated, it is written by an admirer and was probably intended to highlight the bishop's heroic chastity. However, the exaggeration must have been based in some facet of his actual behaviors that appeared extraordinary.

7. "Adam non est seductus, mulier autem seducta in praevaricatione fuit."

8. Trueblood's translation: "close contact that comes of proximity." Also in annotations to *Answer*, trans. Electa Arenal and Amanda Powell, 133: "This phrase emphasizing spoilage caused by repeated close contact (*manoseo*) is an arrestingly physical and popular term in this context."

9. Salceda, OC 4:658.

10. "Similiter et mulieres in habitu ornato, cum verecundia et sobrietate ornantes . . ."

11. Salceda, "corrects" the text from "decencia," i.e. decency, to "docencia" teaching, and Trueblood follows him in his translation. It seems, given the context and the point of the paragraph, that decency or lack of it is the topic.

12. The double meaning of blasfemar: to blaspheme, and to rail against, allow Juana another hidden reference to Titus 2, 5 which reads "ut non blasphemetur verbum Dei." The implication being of course that those who choose the first, and do not admit the second text as supportive of her position are going against the word of God. Also, in her portrait of Jesus she quotes the Pharisees saying: "De bono opere non lapidamus te, sed de blasphemia." We do not want to stone you because of a good work, but because of blasphemy (Jn 12, 32–33).

13. Franco, "Sor Juana Explores," 44.

14. Leonard, *Baroque Times*, 4–12 and 15–16. Leonard recreates one such procession from the first decade of the seventeenth century in his portrat of Fray García Guerra, one of the archbishops of Mexico City who was also viceroy for a time.

10: FAME AND FATE

1. Capitalized in the original.
2. Salceda, OC 4:436.
3. Méndez Plancarte, OC 2:432.
4. To which Salceda remarks cautiously, "No improbable allusion, at least subconsciously to what Sor Juana had to suffer as beautiful and learned" (OC 2:435).
5. Paz, *Sor Juana*, 175. See also Elías Trabulse, "La *Rosa de Alexandría*: una querella secreta de Sor Juana?" in Poot Herrera, *And Different*, 209–14.
6. Bénnassy–Berling, *Humanismo*, 177.
7. Paz, *Sor Juana*, 596.
8. Ibid., 601.
9. Margaret R. Miles, *Carnal Knowing: Female Nakedness and Religious Meaning in the Christian West* (Boston: Beacon Press, 1989), 170.
10. Ibid., xiv.
11. Paz, *Sor Juana*, 238 has argued that it should be dated 1680–88, during the period of Sor Juana's friendship with the countess of Paredes. Although he admits this supposition is "highly speculative," since the date first associated with the painting was 1713.
12. Marcus Burke, "Sor Juana Inés de la Cruz, attributed to Juan de Miranda," in *Mexico: Splendors of Thirty Centuries*, ed. John P. O'Neill (New York: Metropolitan Museum of Art Press, 1990), 354.
13. Burke, "Escudo: The Virgin, Christ Child, and Saints. Attributed to Andrés or Luis de la Vega Lagarto," in *Mexico*, 306.
14. Paz, *Sor Juana*, 272–73.
15. Ibid., 234.
16. The Philadelphia Museum dates it as "eighteenth century." Francisco de la Maza considers the nineteenth century a possibility. See Paz, *Sor Juana*, 234.
17. Ibid., 432.

Index